Blackstone's Guide to
BECOMING A SOLICITOR

OXFORD
UNIVERSITY PRESS

Great Clarendon Street, Oxford OX2 6DP

Oxford University Press is a department of the University of Oxford.
It furthers the University's objective of excellence in research, scholarship,
and education by publishing worldwide in

Oxford New York

Auckland Bangkok Buenos Aires Cape Town Chennai
Dar es Salaam Delhi Hong Kong Istanbul Karachi Kolkata
Kuala Lumpur Madrid Melbourne Mexico City Mumbai Nairobi
São Paulo Shanghai Taipei Tokyo Toronto

Oxford is a registered trade mark of Oxford University Press
in the UK and in certain other countries

Published in the United States
by Oxford University Press Inc., New York

A Blackstone Press Book

British Library Cataloguing in Publications Data

A record for this book is available from the British Library

Library of Congress Cataloguing in Publications Data

Data applied for

ISBN 1-84174-122-1

3 5 7 9 10 8 6 4 2

Typset by Montage Studios Limited, Horsmonden, Kent
Printed in Great Britain
on acid-free paper by
Biddles Limtied, King's Lynn

Blackstone's Guide to Becoming a Solicitor

Nicola Laver

OXFOR
UNIVERSITY

Contents

Panel of the Law Society   5.12 The Professional Skills Course   5.13 What if my firm sues me for negligence?   5.14 Qualifying   5.15 The Young Solicitors' Group

Foreword

Susannah Haan
Immediate Past Chair of the national Trainee Solicitors' Group

I am very pleased to have been asked to write the foreword to this book. Solicitors unfortunately do not always receive the best press and there are many misconceptions about what life in the law is really like. There is a great disparity both in terms of salaries and in terms of the type of work between what are usually known as high street and commercial firms and between these and the in-house opportunities which are becoming increasingly popular.

It is very important that you do your research properly before you make the choices which will affect your future career and before you commit yourself to the large debts which are so much now a part of student lawyers' life. Do use as many contacts as possible to find out as much as you can, from past graduates of your university, friends, family etc., in order to start planning your career early. This book, having been written by someone who has just had practical experience of the difficulties of getting into the profession, will play an important part in giving you the sort of information you need to plan the first stages of your legal career.

I was fortunate enough last year to chair the national Trainee Solicitors' Group (TSG) and to have the opportunity to meet a lot of students and trainees from very different backgrounds. A common complaint that I heard was the difficulty of obtaining accurate information about what life in the law is really like. Getting into the legal profession in recent years has not been easy. Although the situation now is better than it was, there are many graduates out there from previous years who are still looking for a training contract. Having said that, it is important not to lose heart if you are getting rejection letters when making applications, but rather to consult with friends and with your university careers advisers to see how to sell yourself better and to try to gain some practical experience, whether by way of vacation schemes, shadowing, pro bono work or in other ways.

Because I got involved in the TSG almost by accident, I would like to use this opportunity to make a plea for support for your local groups. Not many students know much about the TSG before entering the profession. It is there to represent all of you and to help you, whether by way of providing a listening ear or by organising local pub crawls, but is only ever as strong as its active members. I hope that this will help to get across the message that the group is out there and that, if you do decide to become a solicitor, you will make the effort to find and to join your local TSG!

I would also encourage you to make use of all the information available to you from your university careers advisers and from the suggestions for further reading or research on the various websites mentioned in this book.

I do hope that you will find it of use to you in making your decision whether to enter the legal profession and if so, how to go about it. I know that Nicola has put a lot of hard work into writing it and I congratulate her on having achieved her goal of writing the sort of book which many solicitors would have wished to read when starting out on their legal careers.

If you do decide that a career as a solicitor is for you then I wish you the very best of luck.

Susannah Haan
Chair of the Trainee Solicitors' Group 1998/99
9 April 2000

Preface

Over the last few years there has been a singular lack of information and advice for those undergraduates and students on the Legal Practice Course (LPC) who are seeking training contracts. In addition, despite the merits and strengths of individual applications, many prospective trainees are disappointed in their search for places due to the disparity between the number of contracts available and the number of people competing for them. Applicants include not only law graduates, but also other graduates who complete the Common Professional Examinations (CPE) course, legal executives seeking to step up the career ladder and some would-be barristers who cannot obtain pupillages. And of course each year many applicants who were unsuccessful the previous year reapply. In the last two or three years, statistics appear to show that the extent of the difference between contracts and applicants is reducing somewhat, but there is no evidence to suggest that any such trend will continue and eventually reverse the situation. In 1997 there were more than 1,000 graduates without training contracts but, at the same time, the number of people applying to the LPC was down approximately 10 per cent on the previous year. There were 4,827 training contracts registered for the year ending 31 July 1999, slightly more than for the previous two years. In fact in 1999 there were *more* training contracts registered than there were places on the LPC.

Until 1996 the Law Society validated an increasing number of places on LPCs each year. A freeze was then imposed on the number of places on the LPC, but this has recently been lifted and more places are now being made available. The Law Society's Annual Statistical Report found that, in the LPC year 1998/1999, there were 6,938 places on the LPC. However, nearly 700 of those were unfilled — a marked difference to previous years, showing that the legal training market is becoming slightly less over-subscribed. This is a strong indication of the financial worries that students have, resulting in a great number of law students pursuing alternative careers.

Until very recently, the Open University had never offered a law degree. In June 1997, though, the first OU law degree was approved. This will provide many more people, particularly mature students, with the opportunity to study long-distance for a law degree. This will have a knock-on effect in between four to six years' time, when the first OU law students will be graduating and entering the competition for training contracts. This will, of course, be subject to other factors, such as the availability of places on the LPC and the extent of the competition for training contracts.

One reason for the absence of sufficient information and help for would-be trainees is that it is only in very recent years that becoming a solicitor has become so intensely competitive. One cause of this was the latest recession, which reduced the number of training places available with firms who were seeking to reduce their expenditure. Today, the large increase in the obligatory professional indemnity insurance premiums is a burden on firms' resources, particularly smaller firms. However, in 1997 there was approximately an 8 per cent rise in the number of training contracts, an indication that the recession is becoming a distant memory. This must be balanced with the fact that the cost of training a single trainee solicitor over the two-year period of a training contract can be as much as £100,000.

This book has been written by a solicitor whose path to qualification was littered with disappointment but also with intriguing dilemmas which had to be resolved, some of which are highlighted in the text. Its purpose is primarily to provide a succinct guide to law students and graduates who are about to begin their applications for training contracts. It also addresses successful applicants who are beginning their training contracts and those about to qualify. The transition from being a student of up to five years' standing to becoming an employee in a law firm and putting legal knowledge into practice is not easy. In fact it is a culture shock about which trainees are inadequately warned and for which they are ill-prepared. This guide leads the reader through each step of entering the profession and at the same time highlights the stark realities. Its purpose is also to suggest the many alternatives available, to warn of the many possible hurdles which must be overcome and to encourage the trainee to become innovative, flexible and imaginative in his or her approach to securing a training contract.

This guide will not comment on existing policies. Its aim is solely to guide the prospective trainee to future success, whether he or she is presently an undergraduate or already commencing his or her training contract.

Nicola Laver
March 2000

CHAPTER ONE

The Undergraduate Years

1.1 INTRODUCTION

1.1.1   Becoming a solicitor: the benefits and costs

As a law student, the chances are that you decided to go into the legal profession long before applying to university to study law. Law is, in fact, an excellent general degree for many careers such as journalism and accountancy (see Table 1.1 for a list of alternative careers). Professional legal training is a valuable commodity throughout the non-legal market place. However, the majority of law undergraduates will be aiming for a career as a solicitor or barrister.

You should be under no illusion that becoming a solicitor will immediately bring you a high income upon qualification. The profession is still recovering from recession. It is true that some areas of practice will offer greater earning potential than others — for example, working in commercial property is generally more lucrative than criminal practice — but the time when most solicitors received high salaries has long gone. The income of high street firms in particular has dramatically decreased since the 1980s. However, if you go to work for a large City/commercial law firm, you are guaranteed a much higher salary than your counterparts elsewhere. The gap is increasing annually.

It is also extremely expensive to get into the legal profession — the average debt of a trainee solicitor is approximately £9,000, with some newly qualified lawyers owing up to £20,000. This has been exacerbated by the gradual reduction (and eventual obliteration) of student grants available for undergraduate courses, combined with the recent introduction of tuition fees. Few potential trainee solicitors can honestly now cite money as the motivation for entering the legal profession. (For options for funding the LPC, see Appendix 7 and 1.5.2.)

Table 1.1   Alternative Careers

With a law degree being acknowledged as an excellent general degree in the work place, there are many alternative career paths that you can consider, including:

- Paralegal work
- Work as a legal executive
- Licensed conveyancing
- The Bar
- Other court work as a legal clerk or assistant
- Court reporting
- Community and advisory work (e.g. welfare aspects of law, CABs, the police, social work)
- Accountancy
- Tax
- Finance (e.g. banking, insurance)
- Insurance (e.g. underwriting, brokering)
- Management consultancy
- The Civil Service
- Journalism, writing and legal publishing
- Lecturing and research (although a second degree or professional qualification is usually necessary)

Non-law graduates are required to undertake either the Common Professional Examination (CPE) or the Postgraduate Diploma in Law (PGDL) if they wish to enter the legal profession. The CPE, the much better known alternative, is a one-year full-time course but can be taken on a part-time basis. The PGLD is very similar in content. The courses incorporate the seven Foundations of Legal Knowledge (obligations (contract and tort), criminal law, equity and trusts, European law, property and public law). The one-year CPE course is very intensive.

Although it increases the overall period of studying for non-law graduates, a minority of law firms prefer candidates for training contracts who have the wider knowledge that such graduates can offer. (The same principle often applies to mature students who, for example, are making a career change.)

At the time of publication the CPE costs approximately £4,600 at the College of Law and between £2,500 and £3,500 at other teaching institutions. However, you should check the current fee at the time you apply. Local Education Authority (LEA) grants to assist with the cost of the CPE are discretionary and, therefore, difficult in practice to obtain. You should contact your local authority as soon as you can to find out whether or not you are eligible to apply. LEAs should be able to provide details of other grants available in your area, e.g., from charities (see 1.5.2). Some law firms will sponsor students on the CPE, but those students will be expected to fulfil their training contract with that firm. Details of where the CPE is offered and the respective fees should be available from the careers department located at your University. Some institutions offering the CPE can guarantee you a place on the LPC when the course is completed.

1.1.2 Applying for a training contract

It is never too early to start applying for training contracts. Bear in mind the competition you face with fellow potential trainees and begin applying as soon as you can. It is wise to draw up a timetable or calendar to follow, beginning with your first year as an undergraduate. This should include all stages of the steps which you should take and should include interim applications for work experience and vacation schemes. A suggested timetable is shown in Table 1.2. Add any stages you may feel appropriate together with relevant dates, for example, the time you may wish to re-apply to a particular firm. Keep a record of letters sent and responses received and any necessary follow-up action that you may feel appropriate.

You will see that there is much preparation and determination necessary to secure a training contract.

Table 1.2   Working towards a training contract

1st year law degree/2nd year non-law degree	• Apply for work experience/vacation work schemes with law firms • Apply for legal secretarial work if you possess secretarial skills • Approach Citizens' Advice Bureaux, local law centres and Free Representation Units with regard to work experience • Get involved with moots and mock trials at universities
2nd year law degree	• Continue with the above stages • Decide whether you really want a career in law • Prepare CV if not already drafted • Consult legal directories and apply to law firms for training contracts • Look into the options for funding the LPC
2nd year law degree/ final year non-law degree	• Continue with the first four stages (1st year) • Apply for the LPC • Apply for CPE if non-law undergraduate • Apply for funding of the LPC • Apply for student membership of the Law Society • Study to obtain a 2:1 or higher • Update CV • Look out for careers fairs
Final year law degree/CPE conversion course students	• Continue with above stages if not already done • Prepare for interviews • Note the summer deadline for LPC acceptances this year • Apply for your certificate of completion of the academic stage of legal training
Legal Practice Course year	• Aim to send off at least a few training contract applications each week • If necessary, take alternative steps to secure a training contract (see Chapter 4) • Update CV • Keep record of all letters sent and *all* responses

1.2 WORK EXPERIENCE

1.2.1 Law firms

The importance of legal work experience should not be underestimated. It not only provides practical experience within a law firm or legal department, it also demonstrates your enthusiasm, achievement and your willingness to work, possibly without pay, to a potential employer. It provides you with a 'foot in the door', with contacts and is an important item to incorporate into your CV. If you were impressive in your work and attitude then you will be an obvious possible choice when the firm seeks to take on trainees, and you should take advantage of this.

Before you start your work experience, research the firm thoroughly, so that you can demonstrate an interest in, and knowledge of, it. Be aware of the areas of law practised by the firm and do not be afraid to try to be as useful as possible during your time there. While you are with the firm, speak to the partner who is responsible for training and tell him or her that you are interested in training with that firm. Determine what the current situation is within the firm with regard to trainees and when the next intake might be. Has the firm fulfilled its quota of trainees for the year you will wish to commence your training? Is it willing to provide you with further work experience? When you finish your work experience, ask for the firm's comments on your work, your presentation and abilities. Do the partners have suggestions for you, which might improve your future performance?

After your work experience (assuming, of course, that you are interested in training at that particular firm!) your follow-up work should include writing to the firm immediately, sending an updated CV if appropriate at that time. Before you finish your work experience, check that the firm will entertain an application from you for a training contract. Tell the partners that you are interested in a training contract and your reasons why. Their response should indicate what your chances are with that firm. Larger City firms have set procedures for applying for training contracts after work experience. Check this with the appropriate department and adhere to their requirements.

1.2.2 Legal secretarial work

Obtaining temporary work as a legal secretary is useful experience to include in your CV. It is an ideal opportunity to do paid work in a law firm and see the law in practice at the same time. Practical hints and skills are picked up and you will learn how the law operates in practice.

Make it clear to the partners that you are searching for a training contract. One trainee was about to commence her training contract and was filling in time working as a legal secretary in another firm. When she left that firm, the solicitor for whom she was working gave her a card. Inside it he wrote: 'If you are half as good a solicitor as you are a secretary, you will be a brilliant solicitor!'

1.2.3   Paralegal work

Obtaining work as a paralegal is excellent training for the legal profession. It should also be borne in mind that it is becoming more and more common for law firms and legal departments in commercial organisations to employ paralegals as a cheaper option to solicitors and legal executives. Remember that a career as a paralegal is a viable alternative to being a solicitor if you are unsuccessful in obtaining a training contract. If you are eventually successful in securing a training contract, time spent as a paralegal can reduce its length. (For details of the principles of transferable skills and 'time to count', see 1.3.) Vocational courses have been available for paralegals for two or three years. You should be able to get information from your university or Careers Advice Service.

1.2.4   Citizens' Advice Bureaux and law centres

Training with a Citizens' Advice Bureau (CAB) cannot generally be undertaken while you are a full-time student as it normally requires two or three days' commitment a week. However, it is a possibility during vacations, and once you are fully trained as an adviser the time you spend working for the CAB can be reduced. It is generally easy to negotiate with your local CAB centre the hours you are available to work for them. Work experience as a CAB adviser is an excellent addition to your CV. Appropriate CAB work experience is also accepted by the Law Society as 'relevant experience', which can be deducted from the total length of your training contract (see 1.3).

Likewise, law centres may wish to use your skills. Law centres offer free advice to needy members of the public, including those who cannot afford the professional fees of a solicitor but whose level of income precludes them from obtaining legal aid.

1.2.5   Free Representation Units

Free Representation Units offer another source of legal advice to members of the public who cannot otherwise afford legal representation. Some universities have such Units, and students are often encouraged to take up cases within the Unit. Indeed, such experience is sometimes offered to students as a valid option in the second or third year of their law degree, and if such an opportunity is available at your university this should seriously be considered if you intend applying for training contracts. It is a very useful addition to your CV, demonstrating practical experience to your target firm and a willingness to get involved in advising at an early stage in your career.

1.2.6   Moots and mock trials

These can be good fun as well as being an interesting way to learn and apply your legal knowledge. They can also be a deciding factor in whether you are cut out to be a lawyer. Organisers of moots and mock trials in universities often ask established members of the legal profession to sit as 'judges'.

Law students have the opportunity to take part as, for example, in a criminal case, the victim, witnesses, members of the jury, expert witnesses, barristers or solicitors and, of course, the defendant. Ensure that any involvement in moots and mock trials is recorded on your CV.

Competitions between universities are frequently arranged (results are sometimes published in the *Law Society's Gazette*). If your university does not have an established committee which organises moots and mock trials, it would be worthwhile considering setting one up and organising a moot or mock trial yourself. Partners of local law firms and committee members of your local law society, or even members of your local judiciary, could be approached with a view to their sitting as 'judges'. See if you can get experienced mooters to sit in and ask for their opinions on the format used, lines of prosecution and defence, strengths and weaknesses, etc. Is your university able to give you contact names and numbers of previous students who were actively involved in mooting and mock trials? Ask for tips.

Also consider contacting the Citizenship Foundation, an independent educational charity that aims to encourage a better and more effective understanding of the law in society. One of its activities is to organise magistrates'/mock trial competitions in schools. As a charity, it will welcome input from law undergraduates. The address and website of the Citizenship Foundation can be found in Appendix 9.

You might also consider setting up mock trials in schools — all experience is good experience.

1.2.7 Vacation schemes

Always keep your eyes open for advertisements placed by firms planning forthcoming open days. These are initiated specifically to 'sound out' the quality of potential trainees. Also look out for vacation schemes which are generally more available at larger City firms.

Vacation schemes (usually held in the Summer months) are becoming more and more popular, both with law firms and with students. It is crucial to your applications for training contracts to aim to have at least one vacation placement on your CV. Many firms offer formal schemes, of varying periods, in which prospective trainees will be given a taste of what real life in legal practice is like. Expect to receive approximately £200 a week, depending on the size of the firm. Smaller firms are unlikely to pay you but this is a small sacrifice in the long run.

The benefit to the student is clear, but the benefit to the firm is that it can make a sound judgement based on the student's performance and character during the time spent within the firm. Some firms regard their vacation schemes as a vital component in their recruitment process. Some firms claim that up to 90 per cent of their vacation placements go on to become fully fledged trainees at the firm. You should, therefore, consider your applications for vacation placements with the same seriousness as your applications for training contracts. However, note that firms are not permitted by the Law Society to use vacation schemes as a formal means to assess you as a potential trainee. In reality, it is inevitable that your performance will be crucial to the firm's decision as to whether or not you would make a suitable trainee solicitor for that firm.

Most firms' information packs will contain an application form for vacation schemes. Selection criteria are increasingly stringent as the competition increases. For advice on completing application forms, refer to 2.5. The deadline for submitting application forms for vacation schemes is between 1 January and late Spring before the Summer scheme, depending on the firm. Check with the individual firm but aim to submit your application before the end of December of the previous year to be safe.

If you pass the first selection stage and you are invited for interview, do as much research into the firm as possible. At your interview, you will be asked about your interest in the firm and in the legal profession. Your interviewers will also want to know what you have to offer that will prompt them to offer you a placement. It goes without saying that your academic record will also be of considerable importance to the firm. If asked, tell them about other placements you have already undertaken or have lined up. Firms will consider your wider experience a bonus — it will not act as a deterrent to offering you a placement. Treat the interview with the same seriousness as an interview for a training contract. At the end of the day remember that the firm is not going to offer a placement to someone they would not regard as a suitable trainee.

Note that competition is becoming increasingly fierce and that your applications for vacation placements should start in earnest at the earliest opportunity. In some firms, competition for such placements is greater than it is for training contracts. However, be selective — decide in which type of firm you realistically wish to train and apply only to those.

If you are able to secure a placement on a vacation scheme, try to determine the nature of the firm's formal training programme, the rate of trainee retention on qualifying, partnership opportunities and the general atmosphere of the firm. Indeed, questions about these issues are worth raising at your interview for a vacation placement.

1.3 TRANSFERABLE SKILLS — RELEVANT EXPERIENCE AND 'TIME TO COUNT'

Work experience may be accepted by the Law Society to reduce the length of your training contract by up to six months. Until very recently the time allowed was one year but this has now been halved by the Law Society.

Up to one-third of training contracts registered in 1998 were reduced in time because of relevant experience obtained by the trainee. If you think that you may be eligible, check this as soon as you can. You should speak to your firm who, under new principles shortly to be implemented by the Law Society, must be responsible for considering any such applications. If requested, the firm must provide relevant documentation to the Law Society showing that your application has been appropriately considered.

If you undertake relevant work experience and you wish this to be taken into account as part of your training, it must be considered and approved by the Law Society after it has taken place. However, that experience must include the exercise of and involvement in basic legal skills such as advocacy and drafting for it to be approved as good service. You must also be able to show evidence of at least twelve months' experience for a six month reduction to be granted. Examples of transferable skills include (as well as the work experience mentioned above) working as a paralegal, and working in the courts, barristers' chambers and tax offices; but these are by no means exhaustive of what might be accepted as relevant experience. If in doubt, always telephone the Law Society to see if your training contract can be shortened.

1.4 APPLYING FOR TRAINING CONTRACTS

1.4.1 Introduction

The large City law firms recruit trainees up to two to two-and-a-half years in advance of their requirements. The logic behind this is hard to understand — these firms cannot know for sure what an applicant's credentials and abilities will be in two years' time — however, this does not deter these firms from exercising their preference to recruit so far ahead. Perhaps it is their attempt to 'cream off' the best of the trainees on offer. The fear — if there is one — is that if one firm does not offer a training contract, a competitor will. This means that if you wish to commence a training contract as soon as you complete the LPC, you should be applying to the large firms in the second year of your degree — up to two-and-a-half years before you hope to be starting a training contract. (However, refer to Chapter 3 and the Law Society rules as to recruiting.) The benefit to you, the trainee, is that securing a training contract with a large firm so early on will generally mean you have secured funding on the LPC and CPE course fees via sponsorship through the firm. It will also make it easier for you to secure a loan with a bank if you require one.

Do not be tempted to adopt a laid back attitude on the assumption that you have years before you start training. You will regret it in two, three or four years' time if this is your approach. It is never too soon to start applying, particularly if you wish to train with a larger firm. The implications are that you must put into practice at a very early stage your careful planning for applying for training contracts. Get organised.

It is more common for firms to recruit no more than two years in advance of their requirements, particularly the large provincial firms and larger high street firms. This means that your applications to these firms should ideally also start in the second year of your degree. (One very good reason (among many) for seriously applying in your second year is that if you are successful it is possible that you will be offered funding towards the cost of the LPC. This is probably exclusive to the larger firms at the present time, but bear it in mind.) Nevertheless, many of these larger and middle-sized firms will recruit up to one year in advance of their requirements, or when the need arises. Some firms will advertise when they decide to take on a trainee and will not accept applications and CVs 'on spec'. The annually published Training Contract Handbook (see Appendix 2) contains all the information, as far as the larger firms are concerned, as to whom you should address your applications and when to apply. Avoid contacting those firms direct as you will be expected to utilise the information available. As far as the smaller firms are concerned, it is important that you telephone each firm before making an application, to ensure that they will accept your application. This will save you time and money in the long run.

Chapter 2 deals with methods of applying, and with suggested formats for your covering letter and your CV. It also suggests ways of recording your applications and the responses you will receive. Before you reach that stage, however, there are various things that you can do to facilitate the process. For example, obtain all relevant directories. A list of the main directories in print appears in Appendix 2 and includes the well-known *Chambers & Partners' Directory*, which is a directory of firms with brief details of those included, and the Waterlow's and Butterworths directories. Not all directories are exhaustive — firms have to pay a fee to have their entries included in some directories, and not all firms will necessarily be willing or able to subscribe. There are local directories that your university law library or careers office should possess. There are also smaller directories, published by various legal publishers, which will also normally be found either in your law library or in the careers office. These directories are very useful in providing most of the vital information you will require in making suitable applications to firms. They are also very useful to familiarise yourself with the firm again pre-interview. They will frequently tell you the appropriate person to whom you should address your application. The areas of legal practice undertaken by the firm will be specified and you can therefore exclude those firms whose areas of practice do not appeal to you. Make use of any telephone number given to request a brochure about the firm so that you can arm yourself with additional information. Check with your careers service what brochures they may already have — they are likely to have those of the larger and more well known firms.

Gain access to the Internet and log onto LawCareers.Net which is associated with the Trainee Solicitors' Group (the full website address is in Appendix 9). This is a free on-line information service for anyone interested in the legal profession. It includes up-to-date training information, vacancies and professional news and is regularly updated. Also log onto the Law Society's website (the address is in Appendix 1) which offers full and comprehensive training information for students and is well worth a browse.

Watch out for firms who have their own in-house application forms (or even on-line application forms) — it would be a waste of your time and theirs to send them your CV with a covering letter. This method of recruitment is becoming increasingly popular with larger employers, probably as a result of firms having to deal with hundreds (and sometimes thousands) of CVs and covering letters applying for just a handful of available training contracts. Check whether your careers service has a supply of various firms' application forms. Otherwise, telephone the firm and ask them to send you their application form. Read the instructions carefully and provide the information they are requesting. It is a good idea to make at least one photocopy of the blank form and complete a photocopy as a draft before completing the final version and submitting it (see 2.5 for tips on completing application forms).

Read the *Law Society's Gazette* regularly. You should receive the *Guardian* issue, published monthly, which usually provides additional news and information on training, free through your university. If your university does not at present subscribe to the *Law Society's Gazette*, request that it does so. If it does not, consider subscribing to it yourself or log onto their website (address in Appendix 3). The *Gazette* has an employment section at the back, which includes advertisements from firms wishing to recruit trainees. Expect to find between one and five advertisements in each week's edition.

1.4.2 If you are still unsuccessful at the end of your degree

If you have not yet secured a training contact, and the time has come to apply for the LPC, it is advisable to ask yourself some serious questions before going ahead. Are you certain that the only career path you wish to follow is that of a lawyer? If you have spent the last year applying for training contracts and this has been done with serious intent, then these questions are not addressed to you.

If you consider that the LPC year is an extra year to decide which career path to follow, or you are still unsure what to do, do not apply for the LPC. The LPC year is tough, the pressure is constant with continuous assessment throughout the course. In addition, the financial commitment necessary is tremendous — the average fees of the LPC are about £5,500, and a year's living expenses will also be required — and unless you have a large personal source of funding, on average, you will complete the LPC with a debt of £9,000. Statistics show that the level of these debts is increasing.

Consider taking a year out and think about the alternatives. Earn and save for a year and this will help you considerably in financial terms if you decide to apply for the LPC. Be realistic. Can you obtain further legal work experience? Do you feel you have the necessary skills to be a solicitor? During your degree have you been able to demonstrate good analytical skills, commercial awareness and so on — essential to being a good lawyer?

1.5   APPLYING FOR THE LEGAL PRACTICE COURSE

1.5.1   Introduction

Obtain the application form from your law department or careers office. Alternatively, you can apply for a form from the Legal Practice Course Central Applications Board, whose address is in Appendix 9. Check the Law Society's web-site as you may soon be able to apply 'on-line' for the LPC. You should also be able to obtain from the Board a directory of all institutions that offer the LPC together with the course fees of each institution. It will also state whether the LPC is offered part-time as well as full-time, and how many places are available. Applicants should note that where a university or college that offers the LPC has its own law graduates, it may sometimes reserve a proportion of the places on the LPC for those graduates.

As well as the usual details, the application form requires you to state your first three choices of where you wish to study and any particular reason for your first choice. It will also require you to state how you are intending to fund the course fees. When the form has been completed it must be sent to your referee who will provide a reference for you, and the form will then be forwarded to the LPC Central Applications Board who, incidentally, plays no role in the admission processes of teaching institutions.

The majority of teaching institutions have up to 200 places but there can be as few as 50 or as many as 600. It is therefore important to find out how many places are available at your chosen institution so that you are not, inadvertently, reducing your chances of a place. Competition for places at individual teaching institutions varies depending on the reputation and long standing of both the LPC and the institution itself. For example, the College of Law attracts the highest number of applications for the LPC. Check with the LPC Central Applications Board what 'excellence' rating your chosen institution(s) has been given; this rating is based on the quality of teaching on the LPC.

It is the teaching institutions which select those applicants to whom they wish to offer a place on the LPC and their methods of selection are generally universal. Usually, it is the applicant's academic ability that is the sole criterion for admission of a student on the LPC. The second criterion to be taken into account is personal requirements, such as geography and disability. It is unusual for applicants to be interviewed for places on the LPC.

1.5.2   Funding the LPC

Mention has already been made of the financial burden that the LPC entails. The Trainee Solicitors' Group is active in lobbying for adequate funding and accessible fees for the LPC and the Law Society is currently monitoring funding of the course. The financial problems encountered by law students remain a major source of concern among legal professional bodies and are being addressed. If you are experiencing particular problems, you can contact the Trainee Solicitors' Group helpline for information (see Appendix 1). At present, there is no mandatory government grant to assist with the cost and very few will find that they are eligible to apply for a discretionary local education authority grant. However, make enquiries — you have nothing to lose. If you are experiencing particular problems of a financial nature, speak to your local CAB who will be able to go through your income and expenditure with you.

The cost of the LPC varies from institution to institution, and is between £4,000 and £6,200, tending to rise annually. The fee is approximately £6,200 at the College of Law. Some institutions will accept payment of fees by instalments. Always check this if it will assist you to pay in this way. The majority of students pay privately, as they have no other means. This means that good financial planning and financial advice is essential for all considering this career route. If you have been working during the year prior to the course, apply for a tax refund — you may be pleasantly surprised.

Alternative sources of funding for the LPC are as follows:

(a) *Professional Training Loan Schemes.* These are the most common sources of funding for the LPC. Major high street banks offer these Schemes to assist professional students and will advance monies at preferential interest rates. Names and addresses of the major banks and details of what they have to offer appear in Appendix 7. If you are considering studying the LPC on a part-time basis, make specific enquiries as to what funding the banks will offer as some part-time students have experienced difficulties with some banks (some specifically exclude those intending to study on a part-time basis). Look out for specific sponsorship schemes, for example, a particular bank sponsoring a local trainee solicitors' group.

The period in which such loans are to be repaid can be spread over up to 10 years, depending on the banking institution. You will be obliged to start repayments within two or three months of the date the LPC finishes and you will normally have to satisfy the bank that you will be earning when you finish. This is unlike the Student Loan Scheme which does not require repayments until you are earning at least the national average salary and in which case repayments can be deferred.

If you obtain a loan to fund the cost, it is wise to accept any offer of loan insurance protection. Whether you are going to make repayments over two years or 10 years, there are innumerable reasons why you may suddenly be unable to meet some instalments, whether for a short or long period of time.

(b) The Department of Employment operates a *Career Development Loan Scheme* which is operated by Barclays Bank plc, the Clydesdale and the Co-operative. It will pay up to 80 per cent of vocational course fees between £300 and £8,000, plus the cost of books, materials and similar expenses. Applicants must show that they are unable to fund the course by other means and it is, therefore, particularly useful for those intending to study part-time. The interest on the loan is repaid by the Government during the course, and for up to three months after the course has finished. The obligation is then on the student to make repayments to the relevant bank at an agreed interest rate. Be aware, however, that this scheme views the CPE and LPC as two separate one year courses. If you are applying under the scheme for funding of both courses make this clear when you apply for the CPE. If you do not, you may find yourself liable to make repayments on completion of the CPE and not at the end of your studies. Information is available from your local job centre and the three participating banks mentioned above.

(c) Your training establishment may offer *sponsorship*, although this may not extend to the full fees. Remember that only the larger firms tend to offer such sponsorships. You will be expected to complete your training at the firm and you may be tied to the firm, by a covenant in your training contract, for a longer period of time after you have qualified. Check whether the firm's funding is by way of loan or grant. One publication (in addition to the already mentioned Training Contract Handbook) which comprehensively provides details of which firms will sponsor their trainees is ROSET (Register of Solicitors Employing Trainees) which is available at your university or careers service. Alternatively, you can get hold of a copy from the Law Society's Bookshop. Sponsorship information is also to be found in *Prospects Legal*, which is available at your university or careers service, and in *The Lawyer* magazine, which publishes a 'student special' edition twice a year.

(d) *The Law Society assists about 10 students a year.* It has a bursary scheme which is limited to awards for the CPE, post-graduate diploma in law and the LPC. The criteria used in considering applications are competitive elements and the financial hardship of the applicants. Applications forms are available from 1 March in the year the course commences, and the closing date for applications is 10 May in the same year. Forms are available from the Legal Education Department at the Law Society (see Appendix 1).

(e) There are a limited number of *scholarships* available for the LPC for British citizens of ethnic origin who wish to qualify as solicitors. Details can be obtained from the Ethnic Minorities Officer at the Law Society in Chancery Lane (see Appendix 1).

(f) *Charities.* Information on charities which may offer financial assistance will be available in your local library, but any such assistance will be restricted to cases of unusual hardship. Directories worth looking up are *The Directory of Grant Making Trusts, Money to Study, The Grants Register,* the *Charities Digest* and *The Guide to Grants for Individuals in Need* (see Appendix 2).

(g) Other bodies that take on trainees may offer *financial assistance,* such as the Government Legal Service. Your prospective employer, whether a law firm or another institution, will give you details.

(h) Part-time students may be eligible for various *DSS benefits,* and you should check your entitlement if you are intending to study on a part-time basis.

With all these sources of funding, check your liability for repayment, in whole or in part, if, for example, you switch courses or give up your studies or training contract altogether.

1.6 GENERAL POINTS

1.6.1 Law Society Membership

You are obliged to apply for student membership of the Law Society in order to start a training contract. The initial cost is currently £70 and enrolment lasts for one year. There is no renewal fee unless you have been unsuccessful in obtaining a training contract for two years after completing the LPC. You can apply for membership by contacting the Law Society for the appropriate forms and information.

The membership gives you, the student, a direct link to the Law Society and gives you the right to receive advice and assistance on request in relation to your training and development and post-qualification issues. The legal reason for student membership of the Law Society is that the Society has to fulfil its legal obligations under the Solicitors Act 1974, under which it is required to check the character and suitability of prospective solicitors.

A frequently asked question is: 'What do I get out of the Law Society for the fee I pay?' On an individual basis, it does not seem that you do get much in return. However, the administrative burden of dealing with applications to register training contracts and carrying out the necessary checks to ensure that applicants are 'fit and proper' persons to practice law is great. As a student member of the Law Society you are automatically a member of the national Trainee Solicitors' Group. You should receive a copy of its quarterly magazine, *The Trainee*, together with information about its bi-annual conferences and other events in your area. (See also 4.6.) Membership of local law society trainee solicitor groups usually requires payment of a subscription fee.

1.6.2 Getting the Grade

With firms having a huge choice of trainees, they can afford to pick the best of the applicants. Aim for an upper second class degree or better. A lower second class degree is not always fatal to your applications for training contracts, but note that some firms, particularly larger firms, will automatically reject applications which indicate a lower second class degree, unless there is something particularly eye-catching about the candidate. Check with the Training Contract Handbook whether a 2:1 degree is specifically required by a firm. If you are expecting to get a lower second class degree, see your tutor and seriously consider how you can improve your performance. Review your method of study and revision if necessary.

1.6.3 The Annual Law Fair

The Annual Law Fair is held in various parts of the country. Major firms are represented and are always on the look out for good quality potential trainees. Other organisations who recruit lawyers are also represented, such as Local and Central Government, the Crown Prosecution Service (when it is taking trainees), the Army and financial and corporate institutions. Legal correspondents from broadsheet newspapers are usually represented and sometimes give talks to delegates. This is just a taste of what you might find.

If you go to the Law Fair without preparing yourself, or if you go simply for a day out, you are unlikely to get anything out of it. If you go armed with copies of your up-to-date CV and appropriate questions to ask the various representatives, you will reap some benefit. Remember that the majority of the firms represented will be the larger firms, and will be looking to recruit well ahead of their requirements. If these are the firms with which you are personally interested in obtaining a training contract, approach them with confidence, offer them your CV, get talking to them and — most importantly — get a contact name from them. Write to them in the days ahead reminding them of your recent contact at the Law Fair, expressing your interest in that firm or organisation.

1.6.4   Law Careers Advice Network

This Network was set up by the Law Society, the Bar and the Association of Graduate Careers Advisory Services and other legal groups in 1997, and includes representation by the Trainee Solicitors' Group. Details are given in Appendix 9. The Network provides advice and assistance to potential trainees on request, particularly through its Internet site.

1.6.5   Careers Advice

Keep in close contact with your university careers office and your law lecturers. If one of your lecturers is the careers tutor, he or she may be of more help to you than the careers office which will have many non-law students to advise. Ask your law department to purchase the relevant directories to be kept in the law department, regardless of whether or not they are held in the main university library. This will give you ready access to the research materials necessary for your applications for training contracts.

After your exams have finished at the end of your law degree, you should make the most of the summer in terms of making as many applications as practicable. However, July and August are the months when the greatest number of applications will be submitted to law firms so the competition at that time of year will be the greatest. Bear this in mind during term time on the LPC, even though the time that you have to prepare and submit applications when studying will be limited.

CHAPTER TWO

Making Your Application for a Training Contract

2.1 INTRODUCTION

When preparing to submit your applications, always bear in mind that there are a few thousand potential trainee solicitors seeking training contracts. It must therefore be remembered that, with so many CVs and covering letters landing on the desk of the average recruitment partner, you must make your application stand out above the rest.

The fact is that with so many applications to consider, recruiters will be searching for a reason *not* to employ you, e.g., spelling and grammatical errors, a 2:2 degree. They are looking for a good academic record, proven communication and interpersonal skills, commercial acumen and, just as important, a person they can envisage being a likeable and sociable teamworker within their organisation's environment. Avoid applications that could be seen as 'run of the mill' because they will be no different to hundreds of others that are seen by recruitment partners and will be destined for the bin. This does not mean going over the top with multi-coloured paper and extreme layouts (which, surprisingly, is not unusual). Your aim must be to make your application as striking as you can in more subtle ways. This is when adequate preparation becomes imperative.

Gear your application towards the particular firm to which you are applying, for example, by addressing it to the appropriate person and not to the firm itself. Sell yourself by telling your reader what *you* have to offer that firm. In no circumstances should your letter of application be the product of a large run of letters to different firms. Your reader will spot this type of letter immediately and will not be impressed, to say the least.

As many firms will consider applications for training contracts only when a trainee is required, many applications are successful simply because they land on the right desk at the right time. This, unfortunately, cannot be second-guessed!

This chapter deals with the preparatory work necessary for a good, individual and effective application, your letter of application and, lastly, your CV. Although it takes a considerable amount of time and research to produce a good application, it will pay off in the long run. Invest your time and effort to reap the rewards.

2.2 PREPARATORY WORK

2.2.1 Directories

Having already written to firms in which your interest has been ignited — for example, where you may have obtained work experience or which you came across at an Annual Law Fair — you need to be selective in your method of application for training contracts. Look at the directories to which you have access. Between them they contain details of a wide variety of firms, ranging from medium-sized high street firms to the so-called 'Magic Circle' (top five City firms) and 'Top Ten'. You will find a brief description of each firm and, depending on which directory you look at, you will see the following information:

- the number of partners and assistant and associate solicitors within the firm
- a description of the type of work it undertakes and its areas of practice
- examples of important cases it has been/is involved in
- its size and the locations of its branches
- the number of training places available each year
- how many years in advance it recruits its trainees and when you should apply
- a contact name and telephone number.

Consider whether you should telephone the firm to which you are applying and check the name of the person to whom you should address your application. If in doubt, it is wise to check the correct name of the firm because of the increasing trend for mergers. In the Midlands, one firm changed its name twice in less than two years for that reason. A telephone call to check small details such as these can make the difference between a successful and an unsuccessful application. If you address your letter to the wrong person it suggests carelessness and laziness. Bear in mind that directories are not exhaustive. One may contain details only of firms which have subscribed to that publication, while another will publish details only of the larger firms in an area which take on trainee solicitors. Selectivity is, therefore, crucial when consulting directories.

2.1.2 Which Type of Firm or Organisation?

In what size firm do you wish to train? Are you interested in working in a predominantly legal aid practice, a commercial practice in a large City firm or in private practice in a medium-sized regional firm? Do you want to work in private practice or for the Local Authority, in-house or for the CPS? It is frequently difficult for trainees to distinguish between the law firms that they see, initially, in a directory and in practice. However, you have to start somewhere.

Law firms vary considerably in size and your application should therefore be tailored accordingly. Large City firms, such as the so-called 'Top Ten', attract the greatest number of applications. These are frequently international practices that strongly favour applicants with a foreign language under their belt. Competition is fierce for these firms. If this is the type of firm you are targeting, great care must be taken in the way you approach your applications. Note the best time to apply to larger firms (see 1.4.1 and 2.2.6). In your application, focus on the area of law in which you wish to practice and ensure that your preference is made clear, explaining why you favour it. As the largest firms recruit up to two-and-a-half years in advance, ensure that you show in your application which year you are applying for. Your application to such a firm will be strengthened if you indicate what experience you intend to obtain in the interim.

American firms are increasing in number in London. Offices tend to be small and work for major US clients. Remuneration is unusually high — you may have seen advertisements in the national press for salaries of up to £1 million for qualified lawyers.

Medium-sized firms, e.g., of up to 50 partners, recruit up to two years in advance of their requirements. Some will recruit trainees when required and you should, therefore, always watch out for advertisements for trainees with such firms.

As their name suggests, specialist 'niche' firms practise in highly specialised, limited fields of law. Such firms cannot generally offer a full training contract because they cannot provide training in at least the required three areas of practice (see 5.3).

Small high street/legal aid firms (sole practitioners, to firms with up to four or five partners) generally recruit either a year in advance of their requirements, or when a vacancy arises. These small firms generally act in private client matters, and many solicitors and trainees at these firms will claim that the work is far more personally rewarding and, depending on the level of supervision, frequently less stressful than working in a larger firm. Salaries here will usually be much lower than salaries in larger firms.

If you have decided that you wish to train in the largest of firms to the exclusion of others, you should consider whether you are setting your sights too high, unless you are confident that you are among the cream of the crop. Even now, many larger firms still tend to favour graduates from traditional universities. Snobbish attitudes among the legal profession still abound, particularly among the larger firms. It is therefore advisable to apply to smaller firms too. Remember that a training contract lasts for a maximum of two years and, on qualifying, you can move on. There is no shortage of work for newly qualified solicitors. See the recruitment pages of the *Gazette* if in doubt! However, it is easier to move to a smaller firm than to a larger firm so bear this in mind.

If you have no wish to work in very large firm where areas of practice can be specialised, you may be applying to a variety of medium-sized and small firms. The training given by different sized firms varies considerably. Training in a very small firm can be excellent experience as trainees tend to be thrown in at the deep end, running their own cases, attending court on their own and so on. It can also be terrifying and extremely stressful if you are not given adequate support. This is not necessarily the case with larger firms where matters are likely to be more complex, requiring the input of more experienced fee earners. Teamwork plays a much bigger part in the larger firms. You are also likely to have less client contact but more supervision and structured training.

If you apply to sole practitioners or to firms which practice in just two or three areas of law, bear in mind the Law Society's requirement that firms must give trainee solicitors training in at least three areas of legal practice (see 5.3). It is usual to train in four areas of practice. Often, the smallest of firms cannot provide full training because of their limited expertise. In that instance, the firm must arrange for the trainee solicitor to complete his or her training at another firm. However, some trainees find that this involves delay, and there is a risk that it will take a long time to complete the training. Find out whether you run this risk if you are in the position of being considered for a training contract with a very small firm. This issue of sole practitioners and small firms is discussed later in more detail.

There are, of course, alternatives to training within a law firm. These include training 'in-house' at large companies, such as the large water, gas or similar utilities. Local Government offers about 150 training contracts each year and the Government Legal Service also annually provides an opportunity for a few trainees. Sometimes, the Crown Prosecution Service will train in-house, but the CPS should be contacted direct as they do not always offer training contracts each year. The Magistrates' Court Service also offers training contracts and details can be obtained from the Association of Magistrates' Courts. Details of in-house vacancies usually appear in *The Times* law section on Tuesdays and in the *Law Society's Gazette*.

It is worth repeating that when applying to any firm or other body, always check whether there is an in-house application form which should be completed. Never send your CV in place of an application form — it will doubtless end up in the bin.

2.2.3   Area of legal practice

In what areas of law do you wish to practice? The largest firms comprise specialist departments frequently utilising a large number of fee earners. Does your target firm specialise in your preferred subject? Does the firm carry out the work you wish to do? For example, you may wish to specialise in employment law and appear before employment tribunals. Does your target firm do employment tribunal work, or does it restrict itself to contracts of employment, advising firms and undertaking union work?

Medium-sized firms vary greatly. Some are specialist firms, while others take on most types of clients and have a very broad workload. The directories you consult should give you a good idea of the areas in which these firms practice.

Although sole practitioners and the smallest firms are likely to deal with most types of cases (except high level corporate work), their work may not be as complex as that undertaken by specialist practitioners. If you have any queries about such firms, these can be answered by consulting the secretary or chairman of the local law society in the area in which the particular firm is situated. If you have access to the Law Society' website, you will find details of local law societies.

Whatever type of work you wish to practise, you will be required to train in three or four areas. It is not uncommon for a trainee to change his or her mind during the training contract and decide to practise in a completely different area of law than was initially intended. It is therefore important to keep your options open and not restrict yourself too much at so early a stage. The following are the major areas of practice and specialisms, with a brief guide to what each entails and the particular skills required:

- *Commercial litigation:* litigation involving commercial institutions. You will be defending or suing companies and other businesses in a wide range of disputes. The litigator needs a good grasp of the law and of the new Civil Procedure Rules, together with an eye for detail and the ability to look at the future prospects of the litigation from the viewpoints of both sides.
- *Commercial property:* the sale, letting, planning, development, management and litigation, etc., of commercial property. A thorough knowledge of land law and landlord and tenant law is necessary, together with commercial awareness and a practical mind. You must be able to work quickly as your clients' needs will invariably require a quick resolution.
- *Construction and engineering:* this is often an international field of practice involving airports, tunnels, road systems, hospitals and so on. The skills particularly required are negotiating, drafting and advising on complex documents. A litigious eye is also necessary, together with a sound grasp of contract law, environmental and health issues and European law and, of course, the law relating to construction and engineering.
- *Corporate finance:* mergers and acquisitions, commercial sales and management buyouts, equity issues and so on. You will see many advertisements for recently qualified lawyers in this field. A good commercial brain and an eye for detail are prerequisites.
- *Corporate recovery:* this includes bankruptcy and voluntary arrangements and, of course, corporate insolvency and liquidations, receiverships and administrations. A solid grasp of contract law, company law and insolvency rules is essential. You must have a good commercial awareness and the ability to deal in particular with the demands of creditors.
- *Criminal:* criminal practice varies widely between criminal departments dealing with so-called everyday crime and, of course, legally-aided clients, and the more specialist departments dealing with white collar crime and fraud and prosecutions by the Inland Revenue and Customs and Excise and Crown Prosecution Service. Clearly, a firm grasp of the

relevant criminal law and procedure is required and the sensibility to deal with people who are under the stress of prosecution.

- *Domestic conveyancing*: the sale and purchase and letting of domestic properties. This requires a sound knowledge of property and land law and a grasp of insolvency rules and succession law. An eye for detail is imperative as many negligence claims arise out of slapdash conveyancing transactions.
- *Employment*: employment lawyers advise on all types of employment issues with an increasing influence of European law. A firm knowledge of employment and contract law is necessary, together with the ability to keep soundly up to date with changes in the law, both in the UK and in Europe. Advocacy and negotiation skills are essential.
- *Environmental*: this area of law varies greatly and can include licences and consents, advising on the environmental aspects of planning and commercial property work, dealing with regulatory authorities and so on. The ability to keep abreast of constant changes in environmental law is essential, and the skill to apply the law to highly technical situations. A sound knowledge of the general law is important.
- *European law*: this encroaches more and more on legal practice in the UK. It needs to be considered in relation to many areas of law, including corporate and commercial law. Research skills are vitally important as is knowledge of one or more foreign language.
- *Family*: divorce and separation, financial settlements, contact and child care law are the major areas of family law. Clients will frequently be legally aided. Specialists in this area will often agree that it requires a particular type of character to work in family law because it can be so traumatic. The ability to be sensitive and patient is vital for your relationship with your clients. You must also be able to keep up to date with the reforms of both divorce and child care law and have a firm grasp of tax, wills and property law, welfare benefits and pensions.
- *Finance*: management buy-outs, shipping and aviation law, capital markets, corporate lending and so on. A good knowledge of commercial law is needed in finance, together with an eye for detail as many loan documents will be drafted and read during training in this field. The work will also entail involvement in project management.
- *Information technology*: this ranges from computer licences, maintenance contracts and development agreements to litigation involving computer software and ownership. The rapid growth of the Internet and e-mail is increasing the breadth of IT law. A firm knowledge of intellectual property and commercial law is crucial, together with a grasp of competition law.

25

- *Insurance:* this area of law includes both contentious and non-contentious matters, including insurance disputes, drafting and advising. Clients will vary widely from householders to large insurance companies. A firm knowledge of contract law is essential, together with drafting and negotiation skills. The ability to read and understand complex insurance documents and statements of case is imperative as is, therefore, an eye for detail.
- *Intellectual property:* patents, trade marks, copyright, confidential information and so on, all involve the law of intellectual property which is being fine tuned constantly by court cases and new legislation. A basic knowledge of IP is important, together with a firm grasp of contract and European law.
- *Personal injury:* negotiation and litigation arising from personal injury that may have occurred in any imaginable circumstance. A grasp of the new Civil Procedure Rules is important, together with negotiating skills and a knowledge of the law of torts.
- *Private client:* this includes wills, trusts and probate with a large element of tax law. You need the ability to keep up to date with the changes in tax thresholds, case law and legislation. The important skills are advising and drafting and knowledge of equity and trusts law, property and taxation. You must be able to deal sensitively with bereavement and other difficult family situations.
- *Tax:* taxation as a specialist area involves personal and commercial tax planning and VAT, including tax litigation. The ability to deal with technical detail is important, as is a general grasp of corporate law and practice and the general structuring of corporate and finance transactions.

2.2.4 Legal aid work

Law firms vary considerably in the work they undertake. Some firms concentrate on purely private client work; others are predominantly legal aid practices. Firms that can be described as 'legal aid practices' are likely to have a legal aid franchise. Firms which undertake legal aid work but are not franchised are going to find it increasingly difficult to take on such work, and they are now tending to apply for franchising. The procedure can take many months and involves representatives from the Legal Aid Board investigating the working methods and procedures of the practice concerned and implementing new procedures before a franchise is granted. The grant of a franchise is by no means automatic, particularly with the increase of firms applying.

Find out what legal aid work your target firm undertakes and whether or not it is franchised. If it is not yet franchised, is it intending to apply for a franchise? If so, at what stage are the preparations and have preliminary audits been carried out yet by the Legal Aid Board? If not, what are the long term plans of the firm?

(Note now the establishment of the Community Legal Service Fund — details at www.justask.org.uk.)

2.2.5   For which year do I apply?

Depending on the stage you have reached in your studies, you should indicate in your application the year(s) for which you are applying. It is therefore advisable to consider whether to telephone your target firm and ask which year it is now recruiting for. You can then tailor your application accordingly.

It is useful always to bear in mind that some firms — and many regional and local authorities — will make training contracts available when the need arises. Always keep your eye open for advertisements, particularly as the time when you wish to commence training draws near.

2.2.6   When do I apply?

The larger and medium-sized firms invariably receive the highest number of applications in the months of July and August. The reason for this is easy to see: students have completed their studies, taken their exams, had a holiday and taken a week or so to prepare their applications for training contracts. These applications flood the firms in the mid-summer months. Inevitably, therefore, the competition at this time of year rises sharply. Bear this in mind.

2.2.7   Summary

Having selected the firms to which you will apply, having considered their size and areas of practice, you are ready to draft your letter of application and CV. Firstly, remember to find out the name of the person to whom you should address your application and what year the firm is currently recruiting for. Second, it is wise, at the same time, to check whether the firm is taking applications. This can save time and money by avoiding sending applications to firms who are not, at present, recruiting trainees. Figure 2.1 sets out the details.

Figure 2.1   Preparation for your applications for training contracts

CONSULT DIRECTORIES
Brief description of firms
Areas of practice
Size and location of branches
When should I apply?

↓

TYPE OF FIRM OR ORGANISATION?
International/US/'Top Ten'/large/medium/small?
Legal aid/niche/private client/in-house?
Properly authorised?
Able to complete my training?

↓

CONTACT FIRM
Name of addressee?
Is the firm taking applications?
For which year is the firm presently recruiting?
Is there an in-house application form?

↓

FOR WHICH YEAR SHOULD I APPLY?
Will firm entertain my application for that year?
Should I take a career break?

↓

WHEN DO I APPLY?
Avoid July/August for the larger firms
Continuously through the year?
Keep to deadlines

2.3   YOUR LETTER OF APPLICATION

Figure 2.2 provides an example of a poor letter of application. This letter is unacceptable: it is the classic mass-produced letter, the type drafted by someone who has decided that he or she ought to start applying to firms but who has not put much thought or preparation into it. The following points should be noted in particular:

Figure 2.2   Poorly drafted letter of application

> 1 New Street
> Greenville
> JT1 2AB
> Tel: (01234) 987654
>
> The Recruitment Partner
> Adams & Co.
> 1 High Street
> Greenvile
>
> 1 July 1999
>
> Dear Sir
>
> Re: Articles of Training
>
> I am writing to you because I am looking for Articles commencing when I finish the Legal Practice Course.
>
> I want to train with your firm because you specialise in civil litigation which is the area of law I wish to specialise in. I have work experience in litigation and family law and ultimately wish to work in a litigation practice.
>
> As you can see from my CV, I hold a 2:2 degree in law and am about to commence the Legal Practice Course at Greenville University. I am available for interview at any time.
>
> I look forward to hearing from you as soon as possible.
>
> Yours sincerely

- This letter was probably drafted on a word processor and sent to 100 firms. In each copy, only the name and address of the target firm were changed — a very easy way of applying which saves a lot of time. Unfortunately, this type of letter is far too common. It is a short-cut approach which is certain to lead to unsuccessful applications and is, quite frankly, a waste of your time. Produce a small number of quality applications rather than a mailshot letter like this.

- The letter is not addressed to the appropriate person. There will not be a 'recruitment partner' at every firm. There may be a personnel manager or some other person. Personalise the letter wherever possible. Check with the firm or appropriate directory to whom you should address your letter.
- Refrain from referring to the old terms 'Articles' and 'Articles of Training'. These are now redundant and meaningless, even though many firms still persist in using those terms in correspondence. You are not applying for Articles. There are at least two reasons for slipping into the old terminology. Firstly, it is used inadvertently. Second, you may be tempted to use it because you feel that the firm may not know what you mean by 'Training Contract' as it is still a relatively new concept. Do not be tempted to use these old terms as they are inaccurate and unnecessary. You are applying for a Training Contract, not Articles.
- Neither the heading of the letter nor the body of the letter indicates when the applicant wishes to start his or her training contract. The person reading this letter is not going to bother to contact the applicant to find out and this application will, therefore, fail. At a guess, the applicant wants to start at the end of the next academic year, but it not clear. Spell out your requirements!
- The letter should be made more specific to the firm. For example, the applicant could have mentioned that he or she spoke to 'Mr Smith' on the telephone and he or she understands that Adams & Co. have two vacancies commencing 1999 and that applications are being considered. This also avoids the 'mailshot' impression.
- The applicant gives no reason why he or she is applying to Adams & Co. except to say that the firm specialises in civil litigation, the applicant's area of interest. Was the firm recommended to the applicant? Has he or she read about the firm in the legal press which prompted him or her to research the firm, leading to this application? Is his or her knowledge of the geographical and economic area of the firm attractive to such a firm? Tell your reader that you are specifically interested in that firm and why. Tell him or her what experience you have that is relevant and attractive to that firm in support of your application. What do you have to offer the firm that will make them take notice of you over and above the next applicant?
- The applicant does not say what he or she is doing at the moment before going back to college. Is he or she on work experience or doing voluntary legal work?
- Don't confuse 'yours faithfully' and 'yours sincerely'. If you address your letter to a named person sign off with 'yours sincerely', otherwise use 'yours faithfully'. If you write to a firm, marking your letter 'for the

attention of' a named person, address it 'Dear Sirs' and sign off 'yours faithfully'. Accuracy and attention to the smallest details are important. After all, if you cannot get a single letter (of this importance!) accurate, what hope have you in drafting legal correspondence?

- Should this letter be typed or written? It is always difficult to know what a firm's preference is. If your handwriting is difficult to read, type your covering letter, unless you know that your target firm requires a handwritten letter. Some prefer handwritten covering letters. Always use the best quality paper.
- Make your covering letter concise and relevant.

Figure 2.3 sets out the previous letter of application re-drafted to take into account the points discussed above.

Figure 2.3 Correctly drafted letter of application

1 New Street
Greenville
JT1 2AB
Tel: (01234) 987654
e-mail: alaw@netzone.co.uk

Adams & Co. Solicitors
1 High Street
Greenvile
For the attention of Mr J. Smith

1 July 1999

Dear Sirs

Re: Application for Training Contract — 2000

I am writing to you in application for a training contract with Adams & Co. commencing in 2000 (post-July) and I believe you may be interested in me.

I am interested in your firm because you specialise in civil and criminal litigation. As you can see from my Curriculum Vitae, I have experience in both these areas and more. Although it is my wish to practice in civil and criminal law on qualification, this is not exclusive and I am looking for a broadbased training which I believe you can offer.

I was first made aware of Adams & Co. from a recent article in the legal press about your involvement in pro bono work. I was particularly interested in your website. You will see from my Curriculum Vitae that I am computer literate.

I have recently been awarded an Honours degree in Law (2:1) from the University of Jonesville, where I will shortly commence the Legal Practice Course. In the meantime, I am enjoying unpaid work experience in the criminal department of Eves & Co.

I am available for interview at any time and I look forward to hearing from you in due course.

Yours faithfully

2.4   YOUR CURRICULUM VITAE

Every person's CV should be drafted according to his or her own personal style. This section is not intended to suggest that there is only one type of CV that should be sent to all law firms. There are books on the market (and which you should find in your college library) advising on the construction of CVs. This section is particularly pertinent to CVs for training contracts. Its aim is to highlight areas in your CV that should particularly be focused on and, secondly, areas that can be problematical and potentially damaging to an application for a training contract if not carefully drafted.

It is important to remember that employers are particularly looking for evidence of teamwork, flexibility, commercial acumen, sound judgement and leadership. These can be evidenced in a number of ways, but you should consider these skills when drafting your CV.

Each CV should be tailored to the firm to which you are applying. You will find that the same CV will be suitable for many firms, but always read your CV in the light of the profile of each firm to ensure that it is suitable. For example, you can highlight the point in one CV that you have vacation experience in a particular area of law in which your target firm specialises.

Figure 2.4 sets out an example of a CV that would appear to be acceptable. However, it is not likely to improve your chances of a training contract with your target firm. The following points should be noted:

33

Figure 2.4 Poor quality CV in support of an application

Curriculum Vitae

Joseph Bloggs
5 Long Lane
Greenville
GR3 7XZ
Tel: (01234) 567812

Date of Birth	20 August 1975
Nationality	British
Marital Status	Married
Current University	University of Greenville Legal Practice Course
Previous University	University of Greenville LLB (Hons) 2:2
School	Greenville Comprehensive School 1 Long Lane, Greenville September 1987 – June 1993

GCSEs				
	Maths	A	Biology	C
	English	D	History	C
	English Lit.	E	Geography	C

A levels		
	English	B
	Maths	C
	History	C

Work Experience

During School Holidays	WH Smith, Greenville	Salesperson in book department
June — August 1995	Eves & Co., Greenville	Work experience
June — August 1996	Long Solicitors, Walton	Legal Clerk
September — Date	Greenville Citizens' Advice Centre The Hare and Hound, Greenville	5 hours weekly voluntary work Bar man

Skills

I have many skills that have been encouraged and developed during my law degree and currently on the legal practice course. These include drafting, research and effective communication. I am fully computer literate and hold a clean current driving licence.

Interests

I am a football fan and travel widely to see Greenville Town play. I am a keen athlete and also play tennis and swim. I closely follow current affairs and take a keen interest in home and international politics. I read legal and political novels and enjoy John Grisham courtroom films.

- For our purposes, the example CV is restricted to one page. In practice, ensure that you restrict your CV to two pages. The reader will not want to read anything longer. Never send a photocopy of a CV — use good quality paper and a good clear type face.

- Keep certain details to a minimum. If you have a wide range of legal experience, do not make too much of any non-legal work; instead, expand on your legal experience. This is where any time spent on vacation schemes becomes invaluable. Remember that your target firm will not be interested in wider (non-legal) experience (unless it is relevant to that firm's client base) but will be interested in legal work experience.

- Put all your education and work experience in reverse chronological order. Leave no chronological gaps — questions will be raised in your reader's mind: are you trying to hide something?

- Generally, firms will not need to know your individual GCSE and A level results. It would be sufficient to state '6 GCSEs and 3 A levels', particularly if your grades were not particularly good. Firms will soon ask if they want to know your grades.

- If you are female and married, avoid inviting any form of discrimination by firms and do not put your marital status. There is no necessity to do this and if your target firm is interested it will ask.

- Under 'Interests', avoid mentioning those hobbies that will appear in 95 per cent of CVs, e.g., swimming and football. Do put anything unusual which may catch your reader's eye. One successful applicant, after having been offered a training contract, asked the firm what made them invite her for the initial interview. She was told: 'We wanted to see what a female traction engine driver looked like!' This is not to suggest that you take up bungee jumping or another dangerous sport in order to increase your chances of a training contract; it is to illustrate the importance of including anything which will interest the firm in you, the applicant.

- When describing both your skills and interests, avoid using the word 'I' too frequently. It can give the impression that you are self-centred.

- Use a separate heading of 'Legal Experience' and describe what this involved. Do not restrict it to stating which departments you worked in. For example, did you attend court, sit in on client interviews, draft documents or undertake research?

- Your skills should include any foreign languages, writing skills and computer literacy, including your experience of the Internet. If you have an e-mail address, put this with your address at the top of your CV (and covering letter). Remember that all the applicants against whom you are competing will have the same basic academic qualifications as you. Use your CV to distinguish what you have to offer. Remember that firms' method of shortlisting candidates is restricted to the written applications in front of them.

- Avoid the temptation to include a photograph — you want to be considered on the merits of your application, not your appearance.

Figure 2.5 sets out the same CV reworked to take into account the points discussed above.

Figure 2.5   Correctly drafted CV in support of an application

Curriculum Vitae

Joseph Bloggs
5 Long Lane
Greenville
JV3 7XZ
Tel: (01234) 567812
e-mail: alaw@netzone.co.uk

Date of Birth	20 August 1975
Nationality	British
Current University	University of Greenville Legal Practice Course
Previous University	University of Greenville LLB (Hons) 2:2
School	Greenville Comprehensive School 1 Long Lane, Greenville September 1987 – June 1993
Qualifications	6 GCESs and 3 A levels

Legal work experience

June — August 1995	Eves & Co., Greenville	Work experience in criminal and family law departments, including attending Crown Court, research and sitting in on interviews. Written advice to senior partner on research tasks.
June — August 1996	Long Solicitors, Walton	Legal Clerk (family and criminal). Drafting legal documents, and attending Crown and Magistrates' Courts. Research and advising.
September 1998 — Date	Greenville Citizens' Advice Centre	5 hours weekly voluntary work (eves/w.ends); work involves giving members of the public general legal advice, particularly in relation to domestic problems and welfare benefits. It involves a considerable amount of research and client contact.

37

Skills

My writing and communication skills have been developed during my legal studies, particularly on the Legal Practice Course. My experience at the Citizens' Advice Centre is developing my one-to-one skills with clients and is expanding my practical legal knowledge and research abilities. I am computer literate and this has been demonstrated during my work experience where I have had the opportunity to use computerised precedent systems and time sheets and to undertake on-line legal research.

Interests

I am interested in various sports, particularly scuba diving and other water adventure sports. I closely follow current affairs, particularly home and international politics. I also read legal and political novels, and help to run a voluntary youth group twice a week.

2.5 APPLICATION FORMS

More and more firms are using their own in-house application forms as the first means of selection. It is imperative that you read the instructions — and the questions — thoroughly and do exactly what is required of you. Be extremely careful about the way you answer the questions put to you and ensure that you provide the information requested.

Plan your application form carefully. Photocopy the form and complete the copy in draft. When the original application form has been completed, keep a photocopy for your future reference. If you are invited for an interview, you will need to refresh your memory and work on expanding and developing your answers in the application form.

Ensure that you answer the questions. Some questions are put in such a way that you should try to read behind the question. Ask yourself: 'What are they really asking me?' Some firms want you to provide specific examples of how you have tackled a particularly demanding problem, how you have proved your communication skills, and so on. Plan your answer carefully and think through the questions and answer them logically.

You will doubtless be asked why you want to be a lawyer. Be honest and original. Try to avoid giving a standard answer to such a question. If appropriate, give examples from your background to illustrate why you want a legal career. When completing your application form, ensure that you work towards maintaining the firm's interest in you throughout your answers.

Keep a copy of your completed application form. You will need to refer back to it if it results in an interview.

2.6 GENERAL POINTS

Following the pattern outlined in this chapter takes time, effort and patience that will not be wasted. It is well worth it in the long run if carelessness, inaccuracies and generalisms are avoided. Always remember that quality is better than quantity. It is absolutely imperative that the spelling and grammar in your applications are perfect. If you cannot submit a well drafted application, what confidence will your reader have that you can draft accurate and professional legal documents and correspondence? By ensuring that you maintain a high standard in your writing and grammar, and by taking care in your selection and research of firms, you can be certain your efforts will be rewarded. If you can, get one of your contemporaries or, even better, a lecturer or careers adviser to check your final application before sending it out.

Further helpful comments and hints for obtaining a training contract are found in Chapter 4, 'The Legal Practice Course Year'. These are reserved until later as they may be appreciated more at that stage of your studies if you are still applying for training contracts. Get the balance right. Firms will want someone with a life outside work. Show that your interests extend beyond the law. This is what will make you different from the next potential trainee.

2.7 KEEPING A RECORD OF YOUR APPLICATIONS

When you have started to send out your applications it is essential to keep a clear record of them together with all responses. Ensure that you keep photocopies of all application forms and covering letters so that you can refer to them later if necessary. Do not be surprised if and when your applications increase to more than 100, or even 200. This is mentioned to encourage you and not to discourage you. It is not unusual to have to send many applications before a positive response is received.

The responses you receive will take many forms and can include the following:

- a simple rejection
- 'not currently recruiting trainees'
- 'reapply in a year's time'
- 'no suitable vacancy' but your CV will be kept on file
- telephone in three months' time if still interested
- telephone for an appointment
- come in for an interview.

Your response to the above must be tailored accordingly. Keep a diary or calendar and diarise dates to follow up your applications. A table to record your applications and so on is suggested at Figure 2.6.

Figure 2.6   Record of applications and further action required

Date of Application	Name of Firm	Size	Areas of Law	Contact Name	Initial Response	Follow up action (if any)
01-01-99	Adams & Co.	Medium	Civil, criminal	John Smith	Re-apply in 3 months	Diarised for 01-04-99
01-01-99	Evers	Large city	Civil, employ-ment	Janet Green	First interview unsucessful	Inquire about vacation work
01-04-99	Adams & Co.	Medium	Civil, criminal	John Smith	First interview Second interview but unsuccessful	None

Positive responses may lead you to consider writing to ask whether the firm would take you on for work experience. This ensures that the firm is aware that your interest in it is maintained. Always keep in the back of your mind that, with so many competing for a training contract, you must strive to make your application and interest in your target firm as striking and determined as possible.

Rejections take many forms. The most discouraging are from firms that return your CV with a compliment slip simply stating 'No Vacancies'. The most encouraging rejections are those from firms which explain why they cannot assist you at present. Some will retain your CV and others will tell you that you are not what they are looking for, while others will say (despite what you may have been told on the telephone, if at all) that they are not recruiting at present. Do not take any rejection personally.

If you receive a particularly 'nasty' or tactless rejection, report this to your university or even the Law Society. Some universities have feedback sheets on interviews. Where a rejection like this is reported, other applicants and colleges are sometimes put on alert about that particular firm. A few years ago one applicant (who is now fully qualified) had his CV returned by a firm. Next to his degree (which he indicated as a 2:2) was written in red ink: 'You must be joking!' Save yourself time and do not apply to firms of which you have been warned.

Lastly, ensure that your CV is kept up to date. Each time you complete work experience, obtain examination results and so on, amend your CV accordingly. Each time you send a letter of application and CV out to a firm, check your CV.

CHAPTER THREE

The Interview

3.1 INTRODUCTION

Never turn down the offer of an interview, even if you feel that you will not want that job. All interview experience is good experience. Every interview will improve your performance next time round and you will have more and more confidence.

You should note that recruiters are not permitted by the Law Society to hold interviews for employment of trainee solicitors before 1 September in the student's final year of undergraduate studies. In practice, this is frequently not adhered to, but if you are put in this situation check your position with the Law Society, preferably without mentioning the firm's name!

If you have been invited for interview, remember that you may have been short-listed from hundreds of other applicants. It will, however, be difficult to tell how many have been short-listed and whether there will be a second interview stage. Most firms, particularly larger firms, will have a first and second interview selection process. Therefore, be aware that the first interview may not be the last hurdle for you to overcome.

The purpose of the interview (from the firm's point of view) is simple: the firm needs to decide whether you match its needs. You have already made an impression on the firm with your application, now is the time for this to be put to the test. The interview is, however, just as much an opportunity for you to decide whether the firm meets your needs. Will you really want to train at this firm? What does it have to offer you?

Remember that interviewing applicants is not the only method of selection. Some firms ask applicants to give a presentation to a panel with the purpose of assessing the applicant's ability to research and communicate. Some firms may also request applicants to sit a short aptitude test. Do not be daunted by these less traditional methods — they are there for your benefit as well as the firm's and are not intended to trick you.

Preparation is vital and you will not wish your lack of it to be responsible for losing the training contract to someone else. After all, only one person will secure that place and your aim is for that person to be you.

3.2 PREPARATION

Given that the competition for places is so strong, you can never be over-prepared for your interviews. Do not risk wasting a single interview for lack of preparation.

3.2.1 Information packs

If it is practicable, and there is one available, ask the firm to send you its training information pack (and brochure if you do not already have one). It may provide details about the format of training that will be offered, how training is supervised, what will be expected of you and so on. You may find this information in your careers library.

3.2.2 The letterhead

The firm's letterhead can be a surprising source of information. It will normally name all partners (unless it is a large firm, in which case a list of partners must be available for inspection at one of its offices). Many will name associate and assistant solicitors, consultant solicitors, legal executives and, occasionally, paralegals or legal assistants and clerks.

A firm's letterhead will normally show logos identifying, for example, a legal aid franchise. Frequently, it will identify which partners and solicitors, if any, are members of particular panels (for example, the Personal Injury Panel), District Judges, and so on. This information can provide you with the basis of intelligent questions to ask at the interview that will demonstrate a genuine interest in the firm.

The letterhead may give you an idea of the size of the firm by indicating the number of offices.

3.2.3   Surf the Net!

Gain access to the Internet and look up the firm. Today, it is not only large firms that have websites. It is relatively easy, and becoming more and more economical, to set up a web site and many more firms are now on the Internet — indeed, the numbers are increasing each day. Even if you do find the firm on the Internet but the site tells you no more than you already know, it gives you the opportunity to impress your interviewer(s) by making them aware that you took the trouble to look up the firm's website. Print off some of the information and take it to the interview with you.

Larger firms have impressive websites, providing information about their involvement in major cases, both previous and on-going, case studies of past and present trainee solicitors, history and information about the particular firm, profiles of the partners, and so on. By studying the vacancy pages of the websites of larger firms, you can begin to get an idea of movements within the various departments of the firm.

3.2.4   Legal directories

Research the directories again to glean more information in readiness for the interview. Check that these are up to date in respect of the areas of law the firm practises. If the directories indicate that the firm practises only three or four areas of law, this gives rise to the question whether the firm is large enough to train you throughout the two years. You should ask about this. How will the firm arrange for you to complete your training?

A useful exercise is to study a directory such as *Waterlow's Solicitors' and Barristers' Directory* for both the existing year and previous years. This will tell you about movements within the firm's partnership, turnover of qualified solicitors and whether the firm has decreased or increased in size.

3.2.5   Method of training

Can you find out about the firm's method of training before your interview? Does the firm have a leaflet available to trainees which details its method of training? When you telephone the firm requesting an information pack, it is a good idea to ask (unless you already know) the names of the persons who will be interviewing you and their position in the firm. Are there any existing or past trainees of that firm whom you can contact to discuss the firm, its training and so on (see 3.2.7)?

3.2.6 Local law societies

Contact the chairman or secretary of the law society local to the firm and ask about its reputation (both of its personnel and expertise). The Law Society will be able to tell you which local law society you should approach, together with a contact name. Any discussion with that law society will be treated confidentially and will be particularly helpful if you have any specific worries or concerns about a firm. If you do not have any contacts within the legal world yourself, this can be particularly helpful.

3.2.7 Past graduates

Universities often have lists of graduates who are willing to be contacted by prospective trainees for encouragement and advice. Ask your university about this. If you are fortunate enough to be able to contact a graduate, he or she may have experience of some of the firms with which you have interviews and may be willing to give you specific advice about them. If you contact a graduate, remember he or she may be too busy to talk; request a more convenient time to talk about law firms and training contracts.

3.2.8 The legal press

Has the firm appeared in the legal press? For example, has it successfully defended a personal injury claim, merged with another firm or undertaken pro bono work for a well-known charity? These are issues you may wish to bring up at interview to demonstrate your knowledge of, and interest in, the firm. Pro bono work is becoming more and more popular, not least because of the public image of lawyers that presently exists.

3.2.9 Mock interviews

Ask your tutors (or, indeed, fellow applicants) to put you through a mock interview in readiness for the actual interview. This can work particularly well if this is a common practice at your college and it is taken seriously by the participants. You must ask your 'interviewer' to put some original and thought-provoking questions to you, otherwise it will not be worth the time and effort. What are the most awkward and least desired questions that could possibly be put to you in an interview environment? For example, 'What is your main weakness in terms of working relationships with colleagues?' or 'What area of law do you find the hardest to grasp?' Prepare your answers.

3.2.10   List your anticipated answers

Prepare a list of your good points and bad points, strengths and weaknesses. It is a good idea to prepare yourself to talk about three good points and one or two bad points and to consider how you wish to discuss them. List your unusual achievements and personal foibles. You will doubtless be asked about something you would not want to admit to, but it is imperative that you are prepared for such questions because they are so difficult to answer truthfully. Avoiding such questions can cost you a training contract. Prepare a sentence about yourself with a view to selling yourself.

3.2.11   What will you want to ask the firm?

What questions do you want to ask your interviewers? Beware of asking questions to which, by implication, you should know the answers. For example, what is the point of asking how many partners the firm has when the directories will tell you? It will give the impression that you have not bothered to research the firm.

Consider asking questions that relate directly to the standard and format of training, for example.

- the timetable of training
- information technology
- a case of public interest the firm recently handled
- the rate of retention of trainees
- how trainees are treated by the firm in general
- methods of assessment and monitoring during training
- support facilities, for example, secretarial support and the firm's library
- the firm's overall direction
- topical issues in the legal process.

Do not be afraid to have a notebook containing your questions. This shows that you are organised, interested, that you have prepared for the interview and that you are interviewing the firm too.

3.2.12   Current legal issues

Good background preparation for interview at any law firm or organisation demands an up-to-date understanding of current legal issues. For example, divorce reform, the recent proposals to change the legal aid system and the recent civil court reforms. Ensure that you have sufficient understanding of current legal topics to be able to talk confidently and intelligently about them at your interview. With this in mind, read as much of the legal press as possible, such as the *Law Society's Gazette, The Times* law section (Tuesdays), *The Times* daily law reports and the *Solicitors' Journal* to name but a few. If you can afford to subscribe to the *Law Society's Gazette* then do so. The monthly *Guardian Gazette* is free to student members of the Law Society.

3.2.13   Authorisation of firms

If you feel it is necessary, ensure that the firm is authorised by the Law Society to take on trainee solicitors. This is particularly relevant in the case of sole practitioners and small firms. It you have any concerns, it is preferable to check the firm's status in terms of authorisation with the Law Society, rather than asking the firm direct — this may be considered a little patronising and tactless.

If you have access to the Internet, you can go on-line to the Law Society where you can check authorisation of individual firms. Authorisation is usually a formality requiring a small fee payable by the firm to the Law Society. However, note that the requirements and procedure for authorisation is presently under review by the Law Society and may be tightened up. Each partner in private practice and each solicitor who has been admitted for at least five years and holds a practising certificate is generally permitted to take on two trainee solicitors.

3.3   THE INTERVIEW

Before you go into the interview, make time to re-read your application to that firm to refresh your memory. As first impressions count, dress appropriately, professionally and confidently. If you are being inter-viewed by a litigation firm, dress in a dark suit as if you were going to appear in court. Otherwise, it is still advisable to wear a suit but, at the very least, dress as you would consider a reputable law firm would expect you to dress in the office when meeting clients. Dark suits are always a safe option and avoid bright colours and heavy makeup.

Remember to watch your body language. Demonstrate self-assurance, maintain eye contact, be alert to your interviewers and your surroundings but try to be relaxed at the same time. Your interviewers are not out to trick you and, although allowances will be made for nervousness, there is no reason why you should not be able to relax once you are in the interview room. Above all — be yourself. The majority of people will agree that the prospect of an interview is far worse than the interview itself.

3.3.1 Anticipate the interview

During any interview, it is essential to anticipate the way the interview is going. Many have thrown away the chance of a training contract by not thinking ahead of themselves and being caught unawares by their interviewers. For example, not expecting to be asked legal questions, not being prepared to detail faults and weaknesses and being inadequately prepared for questions such as, 'why should we employ *you*?' Be properly prepared.

3.3.2 The setting of the interview

Interviews can vary considerably in format and situation. One may be a formal meeting with two partners, while the next may be in a more informal setting with, for example, the personnel manager. One might be a very intensive interview with many legal questions, while the other may take the form of a general chat about you, the candidate, and the firm generally. Be aware of these possible differences so that you are not thrown off-balance by the unexpected.

When you enter the interview room you should be able to tell how formal or otherwise your interview will be. From this, you may be able to determine whether or not the firm also has a second interview stage. On the other hand, it may well be apparent that this is a very formal interview which will lead either to a rejection or to a job offer. This is not to suggest that the more informal the setting, the less effort you should put into the interview. Whether formal or informal, you must do your utmost to sell yourself at this interview, making that extra effort to set yourself apart from the other interviewees. Ask yourself, 'What have I to offer this firm that no one else has?' and tell them!

3.3.3 The format and content of the interview

Consider what your interview for a training contract might involve:

- standard interview format
- incorporating a list of legal questions
- a general conversation about you and the firm
- asking you to take your interviewers through your CV
- expecting you to interview the firm.

3.3.3.1 The Standard Interview

There is always a limited number of questions that your interviewer can ask you in the time available. However, there are many ways in which those questions can be put to you. Do not be thrown off course at the very start if you are asked an open question, such as: 'Tell us about yourself.' The purpose of such a question may be to put you at ease by getting you to talk generally so that your interviewers can begin to form an impression of you. Take advantage of open questions to display your confidence by considering, beforehand, how you will respond. Use such a question to your advantage by aiming to set the agenda. Stress positive points, such as why you are particularly interested in this firm and what you have to offer them, and prepare some interesting questions about the firm. Resist the temptation to regurgitate any brochure you have read or the contents of legal directories in an effort to demonstrate your knowledge of the firm. Be original.

Try not to feel that it is exclusively you who is being interviewed. Assuming that you will have some questions to ask the firm (which you should!) then you are in fact also interviewing the firm! If you look at your interview in this way, this should increase your confidence and will show the firm that you are genuinely interested in it and that you have your own agenda to be satisfied if you are going to consider joining this firm. You will, therefore, give the firm the impression that you will not accept any contract from a firm which does not measure up to your expectations. You will also be demonstrating your interviewing skills, and you will most certainly stand out from among the other interviewees. One of the author's lecturers once told her that he had never gone for an interview and not been offered the job. When asked how he had managed this, he said he always went to his interviews with the attitude that he was going to interview the prospective employer and not the other way round! Be confident in yourself and do not sell yourself short.

When you can, take the time to anticipate in which direction your interview might flow. Most interviews are predictable and follow a similar pattern. This is one occasion when your preparation will really pay off. Note down your planned answers to all predictable questions. For example, why do you want to train with this firm and what do you have to offer?

Beware of more personal questions such as: 'What are your bad points?' How will you answer such a question? Do not be afraid to be truthful. One trainee was not offered a training contract after the interview. The personnel manager who interviewed her along with the senior partner was very encouraging when she asked why she had not been successful. She was told that her only downfall was her answer when asked: 'What are your faults?' The trainee's answer was: 'Oh, I have lots of faults just like anyone else', and she did not mention anything specific. Do not evade the questions, answer as specifically as possible and avoid generalisations. Your interviewer is looking for honesty, and by acknowledging your faults you are demonstrating your honesty and willingness to divulge them to your potential employer. It also proves to your interviewer that you are able to answer a sensitive question constructively and openly.

It is important to remember that given the comparatively new method of training, your interviewers may not be familiar with the regime. Their memories are of Law Society finals, articles and articled clerks. Many 'old school' solicitors are not even sure how long it takes to train today! If it becomes an issue at your interview, you can take the opportunity to explain the new training procedure and that trainees must now take and pass the compulsory Professional Skills Course during the training contract. Some firms will not be aware that it is their duty to pay the course fee.

It is debatable whether or not to ask about salary at your first interview. If in doubt always leave such questions until you have been offered the job and you wish to discuss the general terms of your contract. The larger firms will expect you to raise such issues — after all it is important. Smaller firms may not welcome questions about salary at first interview. At the end of your interview, ask when you are likely to hear from the firm as this shows that you are still interested in the job.

3.3.3.2 Legal questions

Some firms will have a list of legal questions to ask you. You may find this nerve-wracking — so will most, if not all, of the other interviewees and this will be taken into account. Questions can include anything on any subject and vary in degree of generality and complexity. Examples of questions that have been asked by firms include the following:

(a) 'Comment on the effect of the case of *Donoghue* v *Stephenson* on the law of tort'.
(b) 'What is the appropriate method of registering a married woman's interest in the matrimonial home having yesterday obtained a decree nisi, and how would your answer differ if she had yesterday obtained a decree absolute?'

Such questions will enable you to demonstrate to your interviewers a degree of common sense and an understanding of important legal issues.

If you are asked a question either that you cannot answer or that concerns an area of law you have not yet studied, there are ways of answering which will still impress your interviewers. Do not sit in silence willing the answer to come to mind, or get embarrassed because you cannot answer. You would not get away with that if a client asked you the question, and you will not get away with it at your interview. Instead, consider what you would reply to a client and tell your interviewers. For example, you could say: 'I'm unsure of the answer, but if a client put the question to me I would tell him that I would research the up-to-date law on that issue and write to him accordingly', or 'I would need to check the present legal position on that point and report back.' This demonstrates confidence in yourself and your research abilities. It also shows your interviewers how you might deal with a client if such a question was put to you in practice.

Remember that no interviewer is going to expect you to answer all questions put to you on the spot. No lawyer is an expert in every field of law.

3.3.3.3 Informal interviews

You may find that your interview is an informal chat, with the prospect of a second interview if you get through the first successfully. Your interviewer may ask you to take him or her through your CV. Do just that, expanding on what you have written when necessary. He or she will want you to fill in gaps, expand on your personal background and talk generally about your credentials.

Basic questions will be asked and your preparation should be more than adequate. Use the informal setting to ask as much as you can about the firm and its methods of training. At the conclusion of the interview, ask when you are likely to hear further from the firm.

After any interview, if you are not taken around the office or introduced to existing trainees, ask if you can have the opportunity to see other trainees. This shows that you are enthusiastic and have a genuine interest in the firm.

3.3.4 After the interview

Within two weeks of your interview, the firm must inform you in writing whether or not you have been successful and whether you are invited to attend any further interview. You will either receive a rejection, an invitation for a second interview or an offer of a training contract.

3.3.4.1   Rejections

Rejections to written applications have already been mentioned (see 2.7). If you were good enough to be short-listed for interview, consider yourself good enough to be offered a training contract. If you receive a rejection at this stage — after the interview — find out why you were not successful. Remember that if you receive a particularly insensitive rejection, report it to your college and, if necessary, to the Law Society.

Do not hesitate to telephone the firm that rejected you and ask to speak to one of your interviewers. Ask if he or she is willing to tell you why you were unsuccessful and what you can do to improve your interview performance next time round. How could your written application be improved, if at all? Most firms will be more than willing to assist you if they short-listed you for interview in the first place. You will be able to learn from this for next time. Partners and personnel staff are generally very sensitive and sympathetic to trainees seeking training contracts, particularly because of the competition.

Although your self-confidence may be dented, always remember that with so many applicants, an extremely high standard is required.

3.3.4.2   Offer of second interview

Confirm in writing that you will be attending the second interview (if you intend doing so). Refresh your preparation and do more research into the firm if possible. How can you add to your questions and answers given in the first interview?

3.3.4.3   Offer of a training contract

If the offer is made orally, request it in writing as soon as possible. This is for your protection. Then decide whether or not you want to accept it. If you are not in a position to respond straightaway, advise the firm and give a final date by which you will respond with a definitive answer. Keep in mind that until your decision is communicated to the firm, the offer can be withdrawn at any time.

When considering whether or not to accept an offer, you may understandably feel that you have no alternative if you have been unsuccessful in the many other applications you have submitted. Frequently, this is a good enough reason to accept an offer of a training contract. If you can afford to be choosy, remember that law firms are not perfect employers and — like any organisation — can have their share of bad managers. Pretend you are a client of the firm and ask yourself, 'would I advise anyone else to work there with my knowledge of the firm?' However, also remember that you can leave the firm after your two years of training.

Otherwise, weigh up the following issues so that you can make an informed decision on the basis of your acquired knowledge and experience of the firm:

(a) the nature of the training programme;
(b) the atmosphere of the firm;
(c) turnover of staff within the firm;
(d) support staff available;
(e) retention of trainees;
(f) partnership prospects;
(g) its areas of particular expertise and reputation;
(h) whether the firm can fulfil its obligations under the training contract;
(i) trainees' and assistant solicitors' salaries;
(j) opportunity for travel;
(k) if relevant, the position with regard to Legal Aid franchising.

When you receive a written offer which you intend to accept, ensure that you accept it in writing immediately. The importance of having everything in writing stems from the fact that your contract will most likely not be signed, or even prepared, until at least the day you start your training contract. Your training establishment is obliged to send you a letter of offer which must set out the basic terms of the offer, such as the proposed starting date, salary and so on.

Once an offer has been made and accepted, it is against the Law Society's rules for the offer to be revoked by the firm. Conversely, a trainee cannot, in theory, withdraw simply because a better offer has been made by another firm or organisation. In practice, the reality is not so clear-cut. Normal employment law rules apply to withdrawal from, or revocation of, training contracts. The questions that have to be asked are, has either party suffered a loss and what are the specific circumstances of the case in question? If a firm revoked its offer the day before the trainee was to commence his training, the loss to him or her will be substantial and that trainee will have a very strong claim for damages and breach of contract against the firm. If the offer was revoked a year before the commencement date, the trainee may have little recourse in law although a formal complaint to the Law Society may be entirely justified.

The trainee is not permitted, under Law Society rules, to accumulate offers. This means that if you receive more than two offers you must, without delay, turn down those offers that you do not intend to consider seriously.

If you accept an offer, ask your firm if there is any preparation you can undertake before your starting date. Can the partners give you an idea of what department or area of practice you will be working in initially? You can then re-read your relevant study notes and undertake further research and, if you are going to a small firm, build up a portfolio of precedents (see 5.7). Larger firms will have their own in-house precedent which you will be required to use — ask about this if appropriate.

If the offer is conditional on your passing the LPC, you can now put all your efforts into your studying. You cannot afford to fail. Continue the momentum of your studies and avoid the temptation to be complacent now that you have secured a training contract.

CHAPTER FOUR

The Legal Practice Course

4.1 THE LEGAL PRACTICE COURSE

When you have successfully completed the academic stage of training (i.e., your law degree or the CPE) you will receive a letter of confirmation from the Law Society. This simply certifies that the Law Society is satisfied you have acquired legal knowledge in the seven Foundations of Legal Knowledge (see 1.1.1) and one other area of legal studies. The certificate lasts for seven years from 1 October in the year in which you obtained your degree or passed the CPE.

In 1993, the route to becoming a solicitor was changed by the Law Society. The old, academic based Law Society Finals were replaced by the Legal Practice Course (LPC) which is a very different course to the law degree or CPE. Its aim is to provide you with the skills and knowledge you will require, as a trainee solicitor, to undertake all tasks given to you during your training contract, albeit under supervision. It is a very intensive and practical course based on group work and independent research, with continual assessment and examinations.

The LPC can be undertaken as a one-year full-time course, or part-time. The Colleges of Law in Chester and York are shortly to implement a third system of completing the LPC, by 'block learning'. The course will last for two years and will take place over one weekend each month at a cost equivalent to the standard part-time LPC. Fees for the part-time LPC are usually the same as the full-time course spread over the two years.

The block learning scheme will make the course more accessible for students with work and family commitments. Similar block learning systems are already in place at De Montfort University, Nottingham Law School and the University of the West of England, Bristol.

Teaching institutions running the LPC require the approval of the Legal Practice Course Board. The standards on all approved LPCs are monitored regularly by the Board and institutions given an 'excellence' rating. Monitoring includes visits by panels consisting of both legal practitioners and academics. Lists of teaching institutions approved by the Board can be obtained from the Law Society's Legal Education and Training Department. Also check the Law Society's website.

The majority of the course content is taught by qualified lawyers who are not usually formally trained as lecturers but, instead, have practical experience in the legal profession.

Plans are underway by eight of the top City firms to launch their own training course amid concerns that the LPC does not provide in-coming trainees with a sufficiently vocational education, particularly in the commercial law field. The LPC is presently aimed at students across the board and the concern — understandably — is that it is too general a training ground for the large City firms.

Trainees wishing to train in the City should keep an eye open for details of the new course when it commences in September 2001 at BPP Law School, Nottingham Law School and the Oxford Institute of Legal Practice.

4.1.1 Course Content

The institution at which you study the LPC will provide you with all the information you will need about your course, and this includes all the textbooks you will require (the cost of which is included in the course fees). The course content varies from one college to another. Universally, however, the course comprises:

(a) compulsory subjects;
(b) core areas (areas either necessary as a foundation of the course or specific to the practice of law);
(c) elective subjects;
(d) pervasive areas;
(e) skills areas; and
(f) assessment.

4.1.2 Compulsory subjects

The compulsory subjects are conveyancing, litigation and advocacy (civil and criminal), and business law and practice. They combine the substantive law, procedure and practical skills. They are usually taught in 10-week blocks and culminate (usually) in a three-hour 'open book' examination.

4.1.3 Core areas

These comprise the following:

(a) the ethical context (professional conduct, client care, solicitors' accounts and the Financial Services Act);
(b) skills (advocacy, interviewing and advising, writing and drafting and practical legal research);
(c) taxation (the principles of taxation, trusts and tax planning);
(d) the European context (an introduction to European law);
(e) probate and administration of estates (the law of succession, obtaining grants of representation and the administering of estates).

4.1.4 Elective subjects

You will be required to study three 'electives' from a list of subjects ranging from the private client to the corporate client areas of practice. If you have already secured a training contract, it is advisable to ask your firm if it has any preference with regard to the options you should chose. It may have already specified which subjects you are required to study if you are to accept a training contract with that firm.

The specific options that may be on offer might include commercial law, landlord and tenant, housing and welfare, child care, advanced litigation and corporate finance. You may well find that the electives available at your college are limited to the expertise on offer from the available lecturers on the course.

4.1.5 Pervasive areas

The pervasive areas are areas of law and conduct which 'pervade' every part of legal practice. These areas are:

(a) solicitors' accounts;
(b) professional conduct and client care, and the Financial Services Act;
(c) European law;
(d) revenue law.

These elements are key parts of your training and are assessed throughout the compulsory and elective areas of the LPC to ensure that you, as a trainee, appreciate the importance of these 'pervasive' areas in practice. For example, the issues of conflict of interests and tax liability should be borne in mind in a conveyancing transaction; client care issues, including client confidentiality, should be considered in every matter.

4.1.6   Skills areas

The practical skills element will make up approximately 25 per cent of the course. These skills, essential to being a successful lawyer, include:

(a)   practical legal research;
(b)   writing and drafting;
(c)   interviewing and advising; and
(d)   advocacy.

4.2   ASSESSMENT

Assessment of students is the responsibility of the teaching institution concerned and comprises a mixture of written examinations, course assessment and the oral assessment of skills. The written examinations are generally 'open book'. The pass rate for the LPC in the year 1998–99 was 73.6 per cent, a small increase on the previous few years.

4.3   METHOD OF TEACHING

This varies from institution to institution. Some combine lectures with seminars and workshops to test the area covered in the lecture. Other institutions will expect you to do all the necessary reading and will simply test your knowledge and skills in seminars and workshops.

A lot of preparatory reading is required. The purpose of lectures is to highlight major areas in the subjects being taught. They will provide a foundation on which your practical work will be based. If you do not do the necessary reading you will not benefit from the practical workshops. As in most things in life, what you put in, you will get out. Although the majority of past LPC students will agree that the course is extremely demanding, most will also say that it is an enjoyable year. However, note the concern among top City firms that the LPC content does not cater for their trainees' particular needs.

4.4 APPLYING FOR TRAINING CONTRACTS II

This section is an addendum to Chapter 2 and offers further advice if you are becoming increasingly desperate and discouraged, regularly applying during the LPC year for training contracts only to have each application rejected. It is suggested that you review that chapter before continuing with this section.

Time constraints during the year of the LPC may impede the momentum of your applications to law firms. Some students will put their search on hold until the course has finished. This is unwise and unnecessary if you have been sensible and followed the advice to keep your CV up to date and you are maintaining a record of your applications and the responses you receive. It is true that the LPC is intense, but if you are organised there is no reason why you should not be able to make time to submit a specific number of applications each week, say five.

It is far too early to despair if you do not yet have a training contract. All through the LPC, students will be taking time off for interviews, some will be receiving rejection letters and others will be offered the elusive training contract. You are all in the same position. Those who have successfully secured a training contract were once making applications and receiving rejections. Although in the present climate, there will be many who will not be successful, do not jeopardise your own position by thinking or assuming that you will be one of those. Pessimism will not help you — do not give up.

4.4.1 Review your applications

Consider whether it is necessary to review your method of application and ask yourself the following questions:

- Is your CV accurate and up to date?
- Does your CV do you justice?
- Do your covering letters require reviewing and amending?
- Do your CV and covering letter read well and catch the reader's eye?
- What areas of the country are you applying to? Are you restricting yourself too much? Can you afford to spread your net a little wider?
- Are you restricting your applications to large firms where the competition is extremely fierce? Set your sights a little lower and apply to smaller firms. Remember, a training contract lasts for only two years and you can move on. There is no shortage of work for qualified lawyers. However, this must be balanced with the consideration of the

particular area of practice you wish to qualify in. For example, if you wish to practice in a specialist area, such as shipping law, you will need to be more selective in the firms to which you are applying.

Some of your college lecturers will, no doubt, be more than willing to review your CV, covering letter and application forms for you and give you advice. They will be able to look at your application from the viewpoint of the practising lawyer. Some of them have probably had to sort through applications for training contracts at their own firms and will, therefore, be well placed to advise you on the merits of your applications.

4.4.2 Further suggestions to consider

- Write to the firms to which you originally applied, even those from which you received a simple rejection. Determination can clearly be spotted and it can pay off. Make it clear in your second application that you have applied before and ensure that you give the firm adequate reasons for your second attempt. Often, success is a matter of your letter landing on the right desk at the right time.
- Go through all available directories and write to the smaller firms, if you have not already done so. Spread your net in terms of the geographical area in which you are applying.
- Look at the Appointments Section of the *Law Society's Gazette*. The *Gazette* also has a website (address in Appendix 3). Use it if you have the opportunity. Do not look only at the advertisements for trainee solicitors. Look for signs of movement within a firm. For example, an advertisement for a solicitor of 0–2 years' post-qualification experience could well indicate that a trainee has recently qualified and moved on. Telephone the firm and make enquiries. Ask if they would consider taking on a trainee solicitor. Also note advertisements for paralegals. You could telephone the firm and ask if they would consider taking on a trainee solicitor instead; and if so, whether they would be interested in seeing your CV. Interviews — and training contracts — have been obtained using such initiative.
- Look in the Yellow Pages telephone directory. This will list local firms that may not have subscribed to the larger legal directories. Many legal directories require an annual subscription from firms if they wish to be featured. Some smaller firms cannot (or will not!) justify the expense of these subscriptions.
- Check your college notice board regularly. Some firms do send open letters to colleges inviting applications for training contracts and

vacation placements. Whenever you see an advertisement for trainee solicitors and you wish to apply, be quick off the mark and ensure that you are one of the first applicants to respond. This shows that you are organised and keen.

- Consider attending the Annual Law Fair, even if you have attended in previous years. Ensure that you are well prepared and take copies of your CV with you. At this stage you will have more to offer firms than undergraduates will, but you should still expect to wait two years before starting a training contract. This is because only the larger firms and organisations tend to be represented at the Law Fair and these, of course, generally recruit two years in advance.

- Find out if any of your lecturers liaise directly with a local law society. Its careers officer will receive information from local law firms (even the larger ones) who require trainees for immediate starts.

- Try door knocking. It has worked for some. Dress appropriately, arm yourself with your CV along with confidence and enthusiasm. Before you set out, select the firms you are intending to visit and make sure that you have the name of at least one person you can request to see. Be prepared to wait to be seen.

REMEMBER: With so many potential trainee solicitors from which to choose, senior partners are looking for confidence, enthusiasm, determination and optimism and, of course, a good academic background. This is the substance of successful solicitors.

4.5 WORDS OF ENCOURAGEMENT AND WARNING

4.5.1 Rejection letters

You will receive rejection letters. Some will be sympathetic, while others will be particularly discouraging. Remember not to take them personally — you can take comfort from the fact that many others are receiving identical letters.

4.5.2 Sole practitioners and small law firms

Exercise a little caution if you have any dealings with sole practitioners and the smaller firms. If you have an offer of a training contract, insist on something in writing as soon as possible. One trainee 'lost' a whole year because she stopped applying to other firms in reliance on an oral offer received from a sole practitioner who failed to comply with the trainee's request for (and Law Society's requirement of) a written offer.

4.5.3 Salary

From 1 August 2000 the Law Society's minimum salary for trainees will be £12,000 (£13,600 in London) with a recommended salary of £13,000 (£14,600 in London). Until then, the Law Society's recommended minimum salary is £10,850 (£12,150 in central London). These salary levels will now be reviewed by the Law Society every two years. Starting salaries for training contracts range from the present recommended minimum to up to £23,000 at some large London firms. The average starting salary for a trainee solicitor is £15,000. All firms are obliged to pay their trainees at least the Law Society's minimum salary. However, if a firm wishes to pay a lower salary, it is obliged to apply to the Law Society for the minimum requirement to be waived. The firm is usually required to disclose details of its financial situation and reasons why it cannot pay the minimum salary. The Law Society also requires details of the trainee's debts and travelling expenses. The signatures of both the trainee and the firm must appear on the application form, which must be accompanied by a set of accounts from the firm showing its profits if requested by the Law Society. Waivers will only be granted in exceptional circumstances.

If you are faced with an offer of a training contract under which you will be paid less than the recommended minimum salary, ensure that the firm is aware of the above procedure. It has been known for firms to relent and pay the 'proper' salary when they realise that they may be required to disclose their financial situation to the Law Society. Use your negotiation skills to agree a reasonable salary. If you are worth the offer of a training contact, you are worth a reasonable salary and reasonable working conditions. Unfortunately, the reality is that for some, the choice is between a training contract paying a low salary and no training contract.

Also bear in mind the national minimum wage and the European Working Time Directive. If, during your training contract, you are working long hours on a low salary without appropriate rest breaks, check whether your firm is in breach of European regulations. Under no circumstances should you be paid less than £3.60 per hour. Telephone the Trainee Solicitors' Group for advice if necessary. Employers have a duty towards you as an employee, and this extends to stressful working conditions including long hours. Your firm will (under new regulations shortly to be implemented by the Law Society) be advised by the Law Society not to require trainees to sign clauses opting out of the Working Time Directive. However, if you do sign such a clause, the Law Society must be supplied with details by the firm on request. Stress and its causes

61

and effects are rapidly becoming a major issue in today's working society, increasingly resulting in litigation. The Law Society is actively addressing the problem by bringing in measures to protect young solicitors.

4.5.4 Discrimination

Discrimination will always exist in the workplace. A large proportion of telephone calls to the Trainee Solicitors' Group telephone help-line concern discrimination and sexual harassment. With potential trainees facing fierce competition it is tempting (and, unfortunately, too common) to put up with such problems at work, because a complaint could lose the trainee his or her training contract. There is little recourse to an employment tribunal for trainee solicitors who are dismissed or have no option but to leave unless they can prove discrimination or harassment.

You can take comfort from clause 2(ii)(d) of the National Code of Training, which states that your firm must ensure that the provisions of the Solicitors Anti-Discrimination Rule (1994) and the Solicitors Anti-Discrimination Code are complied with. Practically, keep a record of all instances of discrimination in whatever form. Keep a note of all remarks made, harassment, physical advances and so on. Were there any witnesses at the relevant times? Also keep a record of any complaints you make, whether directly to the offender or higher up. You may find that this evidence is crucial at a later date. Consider speaking to your local law society. They are there to help people in this position.

If you are faced with discrimination and the situation becomes unmanageable, you have at least three options. Firstly, check the terms of your contract. Does it provide you with any protection and/or recourse, e.g., to an employment tribunal? Secondly, check the up-to-date employment law. Thirdly, telephone Janet Ruane at the office for the Supervision of Solicitors (Appendix 1) and, if necessary, the Trainee Solicitors' Group and ask for help. If appropriate you can also contact the Law Society and the Association of African Caribbean and Asian Lawyers. If you have access, check the Law Society's website for advice.

It is also important to remember that if you have achieved a training contract, you have what it takes to succeed in the face of discrimination. Do not put up with discrimination in any form — tackle it with help.

4.6 THE TRAINEE SOLICITORS' GROUP

As a student on the CPE or LPC, you will automatically be a member of the Trainee Solicitors' Group (TSG) of England and Wales. The TSG is supported by the Law Society. It has approximately 35,000 members countrywide. You will remain a member until you have been qualified for more than one year, unless you are unsuccessful in applying for a training contract, in which case you will remain a member if you have completed the LPC in the past two years.

The TSG aims to promote the interests of its members, for example, by challenging the high costs of the LPC, and to further and maintain a good working relationship between trainees and their employers. The national TSG organises conferences and 'skills days' and produces a quarterly magazine. The TSG's social and educational events, held countrywide, are well advertised in the *Law Society's Gazette* and more information about local TSGs can be obtained from the TSG liaison officer. Local groups organise social events such as pub crawls, balls and quizzes and are well worth getting involved in. The members of the committee are always on hand to assist in your problems and provide advice when needed. However, bear in mind the demands of TSG work in addition to their full-time work.

The TSG has a network of volunteers whom you can contact with particular problems and who will help you find a solution. The TSG can help with finding a training contract, problems during your training contract, problems when newly qualified, debt and money advice and student issues. The TSG can be approached for an up-to-date list of the appropriate volunteers you can contact with particular problems. Over the past two years, calls to the TSG help-line have doubled, reflecting both their success and the problems that exist in the workplace. The help-line has become a victim of its own success with the rapid increase in calls and, as a result, the TSG is lobbying the Law Society to set up a formal advice service staffed by properly trained full-time workers. Contact addresses and phone numbers are listed in Appendix 1. Calls of a general nature should be made to the TSG liaison officer.

4.7 WHEN YOU CONTINUE WITHOUT SUCCESS

It is not yet time to give up in despair. Maintain the momentum of the number of applications you send out. Aim for a distinction in the LPC. If you complete the LPC but are still without an offer of a training contract, spend your first few days after the course finishes visiting firms with your CV. Also consider the following:

4.7.1 Relevant experience

Try to get additional relevant experience — consider applying for training with the Citizens' Advice Bureau. Other legal work experience can also be recognised by the Law Society's Training Committee as 'time to count', such as working in:

(a) magistrates' courts and county courts;
(b) voluntary legal advice bodies, such as local advice centres;
(c) tax offices;
(d) chartered accountants' offices;
(e) patent offices;
(f) local authorities;
(g) health authorities;
(h) central government;
(i) barristers' chambers; and
(j) law firms as a legal assistant or legal secretary.

4.7.2   Training courses

Central Law Training (CLT) and Business Legal Support (BLS), among others, run courses lasting between three hours and one week. These provide the Continuing Professional Development which every solicitor is now obliged to complete each year. Some trainees who are seeking training contracts enrol on these courses to keep up to date with legislation and legal practice and because it strengthens their CV. These courses can be costly, however, starting from around £180 + VAT for three hours. Details of CLT and BLS can be found in Appendix 9.

4.7.3   Paralegal and secretarial work

Look for advertisements for paralegals. More and more such vacancies are advertised in the legal and local press and should be considered not only as suitable work experience to help get a training contract, but also as a possible alternative career. More importantly, time spent as a paralegal can reduce the length of any subsequent training contract by up to six months by virtue of the 'time to count' provisions. Remember you must have had 12 months' experience to be considered for a reduction in the length of your training contract.

If you possess good secretarial skills, these can be very useful in getting your foot in the door for legal work. If necessary, improve those skills. Visit two or three reputable secretarial agencies and ask if they have any law firms on their books. If they have, tell them that is your first choice of employer for secretarial work. This is an excellent and proven way of increasing your chances of obtaining a training contract. Make sure the firm knows of your qualifications and that you are searching for a training contract. Your initiative and determination will pay off and this will spark their interest in you.

4.8   THE LEGAL PRACTICE COURSE CERTIFICATE

When you have completed the LPC you will, of course, be given a certificate. However, if you are still, at this point, searching for a training contract, bear in mind the following.

If a firm is faced with the choice of a trainee who is fresh out of the LPC and a trainee who completed the LPC a year ago, it is reasonable to assume that they are more likely to recruit the trainee who completed the LPC more recently. If you are in this situation, is there any experience you can offer the firm to compensate for the time that has passed since you completed the LPC? If so, do not fail to make it known. If *not*, get some more experience!

Above all, remember that if you are one of the law graduates who cannot secure a training contract, a law degree is one of the best general degrees to possess and there are alternative careers you can and should consider.

CHAPTER FIVE

The Training Contract

5.1 INTRODUCTION

Even if you have not yet secured a training contract, reading this chapter should increase your enthusiasm and give you added confidence in your applications to law firms.

When the Law Society replaced the Law Society Finals with the LPC, it also replaced the term 'Articles' with 'training contract'. The training contract, combined with the Professional Skills Course, is the final stage in qualifying as a solicitor. The full-time contract lasts for two years, but you can serve under a training contract for a period of up to four years, so long as the total time spent under the contract is no less than the total time that would be spent under a full-time training contract.

The format of training varies between firms and employers. Most firms train on the basis of four six-month stints in different departments, generally referred to as 'seats'. Sometimes firms train on the basis of six seats, other firms 'mix' two or three areas of practice together, such as litigation and matrimonial, and conveyancing and probate. On the job training is provided on each seat, and supervision and training must be given by a solicitor with at least five years' post-qualification experience. Your training will be monitored within your firm and your trainers will assist you in managing your workload. Your firm is, in turn, answerable to the Law Society's Legal Education and Training Department.

5.2 THE CONTRACT

The actual contract is in standard form and is available from the Law Society's Legal Education and Training Department. It is reproduced in Appendix 4. Firms are not permitted to exclude any terms of the contract. They are permitted to add clauses to the contract, but where there is a conflict the Law Society's standard form contract prevails.

The contract details the obligations of the training institution towards its trainee. Firms must comply with the Law Society's Training Code during training. The Code sets out the obligations of the training establishment to provide a desk and adequate secretarial support for trainees. It must also provide a system for monitoring and supervising the training and performance of trainee solicitors.

Training establishments have obligations under the Code to grant trainees paid study leave to attend the compulsory Professional Skills Course and pay the course fees and the trainee's reasonable expenses. A Training Principal will be appointed who will have the overall responsibility for overseeing the training. The Law Society must be notified of the name of the Training Principal.

5.3 AREAS OF PRACTICE

The Law Society has recently implemented the requirement that trainee solicitors receive proper training in at least three areas of practice. The areas include the following:

Banking	Intellectual Property
Civil Litigation	Local Government
Commercial Law	Magisterial Law
Company	Planning
Construction	Property
Criminal Litigation	Shipping and Airways
Employment	Tax and Financial Planning
EC Law	Trusts
Family	Welfare
Immigration	Wills and Probate
Insolvency	

This list was exhaustive but is no longer so. Bear this in mind when reading the standard form training contract (Appendix 4).

If your firm cannot provide training in at least three topics, it must make suitable arrangements for you to be seconded to another firm to obtain the necessary experience and training. Employers must give experience in the basic skills such as research, interviewing and communication, advising, negotiating and advocacy and drafting. Training must also be given in practice support skills and experience provided in dispute resolution and case management.

The content of and training under training contracts are currently under review and some changes may be implemented in the near future. Contact the Law Society if necessary.

5.4   REGISTERING YOUR TRAINING CONTRACT

When you and your employer have signed the contract it must be registered with the Law Society for a fee (payable by your firm) within 28 days of its execution. Ensure that this is done because failure to do so may cause you later difficulties and, possibly, invalidate the two-year period of training. You will know when the contract has been registered because you will receive a letter from the Law Society confirming the registration and confirming the date your contract started and finishes. Once registered, you will also automatically receive the *Law Society's Gazette.*

If you do not receive a letter of confirmation within six weeks of signing the contract, telephone the Law Society to check that an application has been made to register your training contract. Also ask your employers when the application was submitted. It is better to chase it up than to leave it and let the months pass. If there is an oversight and your contract is not registered, whether or not the Law Society will permit you to qualify at the end of your two years of training is entirely within its discretion.

5.5   STARTING YOUR TRAINING CONTRACT

Your firm will show you the basic office procedures when you start. Ensure that you understand and become familiar with the way your firm works. Administrative procedures vary considerably between firms and it is important to grasp those of your firm as soon as possible.

How you spend your first few weeks again varies between firms. You may be expected to read files, sit in on interviews with clients, undertake research and go to court with another solicitor. Much can be learnt by 'tailing' a qualified person. On the other hand, you may be thrown in at the deep end, for example, exchanging contracts on a sale or purchase of property, taking detailed witness statements and attending conferences with counsel.

As far as litigation is concerned, ask for opportunities for advocacy such as representing a client in chambers. Ask for time to go to court to sit behind counsel instead of a qualified person. This has the added advantage to the firm of freeing up the fee earner to do other fee earning work instead of, perhaps unnecessarily, sitting in court.

5.6 TERMINATION OF THE CONTRACT

Before the end of your training contract, the Law Society can terminate the contract if it sees fit — for example, if circumstances are such that it has decided you are not a fit and proper person to practise as a solicitor. The contract can also be terminated by the mutual consent of both parties to the contract. Sometimes there is a breakdown in the relationship between firm and trainee to the point where the situation becomes untenable. In such a situation the trainee or firm may wish to terminate the contract. If the other party does *not* wish to terminate the contract, the other party may apply to the Law Society to intervene. This can provide useful protection for the trainee — the firm cannot unilaterally terminate the contract on a whim. Also bear in mind the provisions of the new Employment Relations Act 1999 which apply to training contracts.

5.7 DURING YOUR TRAINING

From the start of your training:

(a) Keep a record of all work you have undertaken on files, including notes of all telephone calls made and received. If an attendance note is made at a later date because, for example, you forgot to make it when the conversation actually took place, ensure that you make it clear that the note is not made contemporaneously. This is important because of the risk, in all matters, of negligence claims. The file must be seen to be fully in order. This means that all notes made on the file must be what they appear to be.

(b) Put all diary dates, e.g., directions hearings, in your diary — and your Principal's diary if necessary.

(c) Write or dictate attendance notes each time you meet with a client or a witness.

(d) Record the length of time you spend working on each file for costing purposes.

(e) Put a copy of all legal documents you have drafted or have found useful into your own precedent file. Continue to build up a

69

precedent library — you will find it invaluable long after you have qualified. Note, however, any requirements of your firm for the use of its own in-house precedents.

(f) When you have undertaken research and you have a note typed setting out your findings, ensure that all references are clear and that your Principal knows all sources of your research.

(g) Use checklists whenever possible. This will reduce the risk of important stages in a transaction or case being forgotten. Some experienced solicitors place a lot of importance on the use of checklists, even after many years in practice.

(h) Make time for administration. Being a solicitor involves a lot of paperwork and time should be set aside, particularly if you are busy, for administration.

5.8 YOUR DESK DIARY

Use your desk diary to good effect — time management is essential to working efficiently in a solicitor's office. As well as diarising meetings and court dates, use it to plan your work, record limitation dates, file review dates, and so on. Use it to give yourself sufficient advance warning to enable each task to be completed in good time, for example, by reminding you a week in advance that you have a property completion. This will enable you to check the file and ensure that there is nothing outstanding, such as the final Land Registry searches, before completion can take place.

With the advance of information technology, you may find that you have ready access to your own computerised diary. Many find these invaluable and more effective than a traditional diary. However, it is important to maintain a written diary of key dates in case of computer failure or other problems. This will help to reduce the risk of negligence claims based on missed limitation dates, court hearings and so on.

5.9 YOUR TRAINING DIARY

Throughout your two years of training it is advisable to maintain a full training record. The most efficient way of doing this is to use a large diary with one day per page to record your work. Until very recently, this was an obligatory requirement of the Law Society during your training. Although it is no longer a requirement, you may find it very useful when you are new to life as a trainee. You will also find it very useful from an evidential viewpoint in the event of any later dispute with the firm.

5.10 'IN-HOUSE' MONITORING

The Law Society's Training Contract Review Group (see 5.11) has recently recommended that compulsory appraisals of your training take place a minimum of three times during the training contract. One should take place in the first year and one in the second year, with the third at the end of the training contract. These appraisals should — to be effective — be structured in order that your progress can be reviewed against specific criteria. This will enable your needs, the firm's requirements and any concerns of both parties to be addressed appropriately and for the focus of the remaining period of your training to be put on those areas requiring further attention, for example, more court experience, greater client contact and an increase (or decrease) in supervision. The results of such appraisals should be made available to the Law Society on request.

It is expected that the Law Society will provide suitable appraisal documentation to be utilised by firms for the purposes of monitoring. Bear this in mind when reading the standard form training contract reproduced in Appendix 4.

5.11 THE TRAINING PANEL OF THE LAW SOCIETY

The Training Panel of the Law Society carries out spot checks on firms to ensure that they are complying with the Training Regulations. Trainees are selected at random for interview with members of the Panel. They are asked to complete a questionnaire that includes provision for the trainee to voice dissatisfaction with the firm. After the interview, the Training Panel writes to both the firm and the trainee indicating its satisfaction or otherwise with the training being provided. If necessary, the Law Society will take steps to improve your training and the conditions under which you are working. If you are unhappy with your training, for example, through lack of supervision or lack of experience, you can always ask the Training Panel to commence monitoring.

The Training Contract Review Group consists of representatives throughout the profession, including academics, Law Society Council members and members of the TSG. The Group reviews the system of training and makes recommendations as appropriate with a view to improving the system and quality of training of solicitors. Copies of the latest findings and recommendations of the group can be obtained from the Law Society.

The Law Society has for some years produced checklists of the work experience you might gain in each area of law in which you receive training. Two are reproduced in Appendix 6. They can be obtained from the Law Society's Legal Education and Training Department. After the recent review, the Law Society will now only be reproducing checklists for nine areas of law: civil litigation, property, family, trusts, welfare, personal injury, local government, shipping and commercial. These will be regularly updated.

5.12   THE PROFESSIONAL SKILLS COURSE

All trainee solicitors must attend and pass the Professional Skills Course (PSC) (introduced in 1994) which can be undertaken either full-time as a 'fast track' course over 12 consecutive days, or part-time. Your firm is obliged to grant you paid study leave to attend the PSC and is responsible for paying the course fee. You cannot apply for admission to the Roll of Solicitors until you satisfy the Law Society that you have satisfactorily passed (or are exempt from) the PSC.

Unless you are training at one of the large City firms, where the course will frequently be run 'in-house', you will have to go to a venue outside your office to take the course. Further details about where the PSC is run are available from the Law Society.

The PSC has recently been revised in line with a revision in the content of the LPC. The PSC provides training and practice in three 'heads':

1.   Financial and Business Skills (including Investment Business)
2.   Advocacy and Communication (e.g., rights of audience, negotiation)
3.   Ethics and Client Responsibilities (e.g., client care, ethical problems).

These components are taught on a face-to-face basis and are assessed either by practical assessment of the skill (e.g., advocacy), or by written examination (e.g., investment business). You will also be required to spend time on 'elective' subjects, expanding your expertise in one of the subject areas. This is of particular benefit both to you and your firm as you can choose an elective area appropriate to the specific area of legal practice in your training.

The PSC is aimed at ensuring that you reach the level of legal skills required for professional legal practice. However, if you satisfy certain criteria, for example, several years' advocacy experience, you can claim exemption from parts of the PSC. Details can be obtained from the Law Society and from its website.

5.13   WHAT IF MY FIRM SUES ME FOR NEGLIGENCE?

This is an important issue presently being addressed by the Trainee Solicitors' Group, the Young Solicitors' Group and the Freelance Solicitors'

Group. It has not yet been resolved but is due to go before the Law Society's Council at some stage.

If a solicitor makes a mistake during his or her employment and has acted in good faith and the firm is sued for professional negligence, the firm may attempt, in turn, to sue the solicitor who made the mistake. Such lawsuits are commonly regarded as distasteful and unacceptable — particularly in the light of professional indemnity insurance. It is hoped that the practice will be outlawed, and that new rules will apply retrospectively.

In the meantime, when you qualify you may be requested to sign a contract of employment in which the firm reserves (expressly or by default) the right to sue you for negligence. The Campaign for Regulations to Outlaw Solicitors Suing Staff (CROSS!), a task force set up in conjunction with the Young Solicitors' Group, the Trainee Solicitors' Group, the Freelance Solicitors' Group and the Association of Women Solicitors to address issues of this type, has drafted a model clause which you may wish to insist is inserted into your contract. The model clause is reproduced in Appendix 8. If necessary, seek further advice from the Young Solicitors' Group about this issue.

5.14 QUALIFYING

A few weeks before your training contract is due to end, the Law Society will send you an application form for your first practising certificate and for admission to the Roll of Solicitors. You and your Training Principal will be required to complete a form certifying that you have received full training and passed all elements of the PSC.

Applications for practising certificates take some weeks to process. However, you are entitled to practise as a fully qualified solicitor from the date your application is received by the Law Society as long as you have been entered onto the Roll and your application for a practising certificate has, at least, been checked. On or soon after that date, the Law Society will be able to issue you with your individual roll number. You will need this, particularly if you do any legal aid work.

Once you are qualified and you take on your own caseload, that is when the true training begins. It is extremely common to find that you really are in at the deep end once you have qualified, whether you remain at the firm with which you trained, or move to another firm. During your training contract, you can always comfort yourself with the fact that your Training Principal or supervisor and your firm are responsible for checking all your work (in theory if not in practice!) and that any mistakes you make are not your ultimate responsibility. Indeed, you are expected to learn from your mistakes. That is why you are required to spend such a lengthy period training 'on the job'. When you qualify, that support and comfort goes and you become responsible for your own actions. It is common for solicitors to admit quite readily that the hardest time in their career was the first few months after qualifying. Take comfort from that. Learn from your mistakes and do not be afraid to ask for help from your colleagues.

5.15   THE YOUNG SOLICITORS' GROUP

The Young Solicitors' Group (YSG) exists for the encouragement and advancement of young solicitors in England and Wales. Its membership is made up of more than 40,000 solicitors who are either under 36 years of age, or over 36 and who have been qualified for less than five years. The membership accounts for more than half of practising solicitors. One of its objectives is to encourage its members to become actively involved in addressing existing problems within the profession, and it is a collective means of bringing problems facing young solicitors to the attention of the Law Society Council and MPs.

The Law Society is generally available for help and advice during your years as a trainee solicitor and during your post-qualification years. Make the most of it. You will find that you are inexperienced for many months before you can feel confident about ethical issues, dealing with difficult clients and client care issues. Make the most of the support services available.

Most importantly, throughout your six years or more of training, keep in mind those things you have learnt from your practical experience. As the adage says: 'Practice makes perfect.'

Addresses and Useful Contacts at the Law Society and Trainee Solicitors' Group

The Law Society
113 Chancery Lane
London WC2A 1PL
Tel: (020) 7242 1222
Fax: (020) 7831 0344
www.lawsociety.org.uk

The Law Society's Careers Recruitment Service
113 Chancery Lane
London WC2A 1PL
Tel: (020) 7242 1222
Fax: (020) 7831 0344

The Law Society's Legal Education and Training Department
Ipsley Court
Redditch
Worcestershire BN8 0TD
Tel: (01527) 517141/(0870) 6062555
Fax: (020) 7320 5964

Ethnic Minorities Careers Officer
114 Chancery Lane
London WC2A 1PQ
Tel: (020) 7320 5873

Law Society Bursaries
Tel: (0870) 606 2555

Law Society Professional Ethics
Tel: (0870) 606 2577

Law Society Practice Advice
Tel: (0870) 606 2522

Law Society Recruitment Service
Tel: (020) 7320 5940

Law Society Student and Trainee Services
Tel: (0870) 606 2555

The Office for the Supervision of Solicitors
Janet Ruane (Discrimination)
Victoria Court
Dormer Place
Leamington Spa
Warwickshire CV32 5AE
Tel: (01926) 820082 Ext. 2284
Fax: (01926) 431604

The Trainee Solicitors' Group
Law Society
113 Chancery Lane
London WC2A 1PL
Tel: (020) 7320 5794
Fax: (020) 7316 5697
www.tsg.org.uk

Chair: Grace Martins-Waring
                                The National Assembly for Wales
                                Office of the Counsel General
                                Crown Buildings
                                Cathays Park
                                Cardiff
                                Tel: (029) 2082 5374
                                Fax: (029) 2082 3834

Vice-chair: Theeba Ragunathan
                       Myers Fletcher & Gordon
                       15 Cambridge Court
                       210 Shepherds Bush Road
                       Hammersmith
                       London W6 7NJ
                       Tel: (020) 7610 4433
                       Fax: (020) 7610 4455

Education Officer: Harjinder Kaur
                       15A Cobham Road
                       Westcliffe
                       Essex SS0 8EG
                       Tel: (07932) 031350
                       Fax: (01702) 331563

Liaison Officer: Aviva Gulley
                       The Law Society
                       114 Chancery Lane
                       London WC2A 1PQ
                       Tel: (020) 7320 5794
                       Fax: (020) 7316 5697

(For further Executive Committee members, contact the TSG at the Law Society.)

Directories

Butterworth's Directory
Butterworth & Co. Limited
Halsbury House
35 Chancery Lane
London WC2A 1EL
Tel: (020) 7400 2500
Fax: (020) 7400 2842

Chambers & Partners Directory
Chambers & Partners Publishing
23 Long Lane
London EC1A 9ET
Tel: (020) 7606 1300
Fax: (020) 7606 0906

Charities Digest
Family Welfare Association, Family Welfare Enterprises
501–5 Kingsland Road
London E8, 4AU
Tel: (020) 7254 6251
Fax: (020) 7249 5443

GTI Career Journal — Law

GTI
The Barns
Preston Crowmarsh
Wallingford
Oxon OX10 6SL
Tel: (01491) 826262
Fax: (01491) 833146

Grants to Students — A Brief Guide
Department of Further Education and Employment
Student Support Team
Mowden Hall
Staindrop Road
Darlington DL3 9BG
Tel: (01325) 392822
Fax: (01325) 392464

The Directory of Grant Making Trusts
Charities Aid Foundation
Kings Hill
West Malling
Kent ME19 4TA
Tel: (01732) 520000
Fax: (01732) 520001

The Grants Registry
Waterlow's Specialist Information Publishing Limited
6–14 Underwood Street
London N1 7JQ
Tel: (020) 7324 2340
Fax: (020) 7324 2369

The Guide to Grants for Individuals in Need
Directory of Social Change
24 Stephenson Way
London NW1 2DP
Tel: (020) 7209 5151
Fax: (020) 7209 5049

Law Society Directory of Solicitors and Barristers
The Law Society
13 Chancery Lane

London WC2A 1PL
Tel: (020) 7242 1222
Fax: (020) 7831 0344

The Legal 500
Legalease
28–33 Cato Street
London W1H 5HS
Tel: (020) 7396 9292
Fax: (020) 7396 9300

The Training Contract Handbook
Globe Business Publishing Limited
in assoc. with the Trainee Solicitors' Group
One Cathedral Street
London Bridge
London SE1 9DE
Tel: (020) 7234 0606
Fax: (020) 7234 0808

Waterlow's Solicitors' and Barristers' Directory
Waterlow Legal Publishing
Paulton House
8 Shepherdess Walk
London N1 7LB
Tel: (020) 7490 0049
Fax: (020) 7608 1163

APPENDIX THREE

Legal Magazines

Law Society's Gazette
The Law Society
113 Chancery Lane
London WC2A 1PL
Tel: (020) 7242 1222
Fax: (020) 7831 0344
www.lawgazette.co.uk

The Lawyer
Centaur Communications Group
50 Poland Street
London W1V 4AX
Tel: (020) 7439 4222
Fax: (020) 7970 4668
www.the-lawyer.co.uk

Lex
New City Media
19 Bedford Row
London WC1R 4EB
Tel: (020) 7430 7970
Fax: (020) 7831 3171
www.lex@ncm.co.uk

Prospects Legal
SCU Limited
Prospect House
Booth Street East
Manchester M13 9EP
Tel: (0161) 277 5200
Fax: (0161) 277 5210
www.prospects.scu.ac.uk

The Training Contract

THIS CONTRACT is made on   20

BETWEEN   'X'   (The 'Training Establishment') and

                                          (the Trainee Solicitor)

1. 'X' is the Training Establishment for the purpose of the Training Regulations 1990

2. [The Training Establishment] is authorised by the Law Society and has agreed to provide training for the Trainee Solicitor according to the rules of the Law Society.

3. The Trainee Solicitor agrees to be trained by the [Training Establishment].

4. [The Training Establishment] has appointed   to be its Training Principal.

DATE OF COMMENCEMENT AND FIXED TERM

5. This Contract begins on   and continues for two years, subject to the provisions for earlier termination.

COVENANTS OF [THE TRAINING ESTABLISHMENT]

Salary

6. [The Training Establishment] will:

    (a) pay the Trainee solicitor a yearly salary of not less than £ payable by equal monthly instalments.

    (b) ensure that the Trainee Solicitor's salary is never less than the minimum prescribed for Trainee Solicitors in the local law society area where the Trainee Solicitor is based.

Note:

   The name of the Training Establishment may be substituted for the wording given in square brackets.

Training Principal

7. (a) The Training Principal is the individual responsible for [the Training Establishment's] obligations under this Contract.

    (b) The Training Principal may delegate these responsibilities to others but where this is done the name of the person or persons appointed must be given to the Trainee Solicitor.

Terms and Conditions

8. The Trainee Solicitor is employed by [the Training Establishment] under the terms and conditions of employment which have been supplied but if there is any conflict between those terms and this Contract then the terms of this Contract prevail.

Basic Skills

9. [The Training Establishment] will:

    (a) provide the Trainee Solicitor with the opportunity to practice:

        (i) communication skills;

        (ii) practice support skills;

(iii)   legal research;

(iv)   drafting;

(v)   interviewing and advising;

(b)   provide the Trainee Solicitor with the opportunity to gain experience of the practice of:

(i)   negotiation;

(ii)   advocacy and oral presentation skills.

Legal Topics

10.   (a)   [The Training Establishment] will provide the Trainee Solicitor with the proper training and experience in at least three of the following English legal topics [this list is no longer exhaustive (5.3)]:

Banking;	Intellectual Property;
Civil Litigation;	Local Government;
Commercial;	Magisterial;
Company;	Planning;
Construction;	Personal Injury;
Criminal Litigation;	Property (including Landlord
Employment;	and Tenant);
European Community;	Shipping and Airways;
Family;	Tax and Financial Planning;
Immigration;	Trusts;
Insolvency;	Welfare;
Insurance and Reinsurance	Wills and Probate;

If [the Training Establishment] is not able to provide proper training and experience in at least three of these topics it must make suitable arrangements for the Trainee Solicitor to be seconded to an office of another solicitor or elsewhere agreed by the Law Society to acquire the appropriate experience.

(b)   [The Training Establishment] must ensure that during the term of the Training Contract the Trainee Solicitor gains experience of both contentious and non-contentious work.

Review of Experience and Appraisal of Performance

11. [The Training Establishment] will:

(a) provide the Trainee Solicitor with the means to maintain a record of the Trainee Solicitor's training;

(b) ensure adequate arrangements for guidance, including access to a supervising solicitor, on a day to day basis;

(c) make suitable arrangements to monitor the Trainee Solicitor's progress and at least quarterly to discuss that progress with the Trainee Solicitor.

(d) make prompt and adequate arrangements to deal with any personnel concerns in respect of the Trainee Solicitor.

[Note the introduction of three compulsory appraisals (5.10) during your training contract.]

Law Society Requirements

12. [The Training Establishment] will:

(a) (i) permit the Trainee Solicitor to have paid leave to attend courses and interviews as required by the Law Society or local law society;

(ii) pay the fees and reasonable expenses in connection with such courses and interviews.

(b) inform the Trainee Solicitor of any change:

(i) in the Law Society's requirements relating to this training contract;

(ii) of the Training Principal;

(c) permit the Trainee Solicitor to have 20 working days paid holiday in each year of employment in addition to public holidays;

(d) complete a certificate of training at the end of this Contract.

APPENDIX FIVE

...acts from the Law Society's National Code of Training

...n 3)

...e Training Establishment

—

) —

...i) The Training Establishment will provide:—

(a) a desk available for the trainee solicitor's own work;

(b) appropriate secretarial support;

(c) convenient access to a library or suitable material for research.

—

Arrangements for Training

(i) The Training Establishment will provide:—

COVENANTS OF THE TRAINEE SOLICITOR

Duties

13. The Trainee Solicitor will:

(a) carry out duties given by partners or employees of [the Training Establishment] faithfully and diligently and follow all reasonable instructions;

(b) treat all information about [the Training Establishment] and its clients and their business as wholly confidential;

(c) deal properly with any money or property entrusted to the Trainee Solicitor;

(d) keep a proper record of all work done and training received;

(e) comply with all requirements of the Law Society;

(f) attend courses and interviews as required by the Law Society and the Training Principal.

DISPUTES

14. (a) Any dispute about this Contract or the conduct of either party in relation to it may be referred to the Training Principal (or another appropriate person within [the Training Establishment] if the dispute concerns the Training Principal), who must deal with it within four weeks of referral.

(b) If the dispute is not resolved within four weeks the issue may be referred by either party to the law Society or such person as it may appoint.

(c) The Trainee Solicitor may also use [the Training Establishment's] grievance procedure.

APPLICABLE LAW

15. This Contract is subject to English Law.

NOTICES

16. Any notices must be in writing and given:

    (a) personally; or

    (b) by post addressed to the other party at:

        (i) the address set out in this Contract; or

        (ii) any other address given by one party to the other for the purpose of this clause.

17. Any notice to be given to [the Training Establishment] must be addressed to the Training Principal.

18. Notices will be deemed served two working days after posting.

TERMINATION

19. This Contract may be terminated by:

    (a) agreement between [the Training Establishment] and the Trainee Solicitor.

    (b) the Law Society:

        (i) with or without an application for that purpose by either party;

        (ii) following an application by [the Training Establishment] in the event of poor performance by the Trainee Solicitor.

20. This Contract would not normally be terminated by:

    (a) the resignation or appointment of any partner of [the Training Establishment]

    (b) the merger of [the Training Establishment] with another body, firm, company or individual

21. If the Trainee Solicitor:

    (a) has completed a Legal Practice Cou
        Exempting Law Degree Course o
        Examinations and

    (b) commenced this Contract prior to th
        of that course or examinations;

    either party may end this Contract within
    being published if the Trainee Solicitor do
    standard as set out in the letter of offer.

22. Under Section 197(1) and 197(3) of the Emp
    the Trainee Solicitor excludes any right unde
    135 and 139 of the Act in relation to the expi

Signed by

on behalf of [the Training Establishment]

Signed:

Trainee Solicitor

Version 3
January 1997
The Law Society

Extr

(Versi

1.   Tl

        (i

        (i

        (i

2.

3.

(a) practical instruction and supervised experience in three of the prescribed legal topics and the prescribed legal skills as set out in the Skills Standards for training produced as guidance by the Society [but see 5.3];

(b) the opportunity for the trainee solicitor to learn the principles of professional conduct.

(ii) —

(iii) —

4. Supervision of Training

(i) Trainee Solicitors will be adequately supervised within the Training Establishment;

(ii) Supervisors must have adequate time to devote to the supervision of training;

(iii) In addition to regular meetings with each trainee solicitor there will be adequate arrangements for the daily guidance.

APPENDIX SIX

Checklists for Training

—Take in artwork — 10 pages—

AREA OF PRACTICE	✓	ENTER A BRIEF COMMENTARY OF THE SKILLS GAINED; DETAIL THE WORK COMPLETED AND THE FREQUENCY WITH WHICH THE SKILLS WERE PRACTISED OR OBSERVED	DETAILS OF SUPERVISOR
CONTENTIOUS		**SECTION ONE**	
1.1			
1.1.1 Passing-off.			
1.1.2 Trade mark infringement.			
1.1.3 Copyright infringement.			
1.1.4 Registered design and infringement of registered design right.			
1:1.5 Patent action.			
1.1.6 Distribution and Licence agreements.			
1.1.7 Unregistered design right.			
1.1.8 Confidential information.			
1.2 Research procedure			
1.2.1 High Court.			
1.2.2 Patent Court (RSC 0.104).			
1.2.3 Patents County Court.			
1.2.4 Trade Mark Registry.			
1.2.5 Patent Office.			
1.2.6 EEC law and how it affects IIP law.			
1.2.7 Drafting letters of advice based on research.			
1.3 High Court			
1.3.1 Draft writ, with simple endorsement.			
1.3.2 Appear before Master/ District Judge.			
1.3.3			
1.3.3.1 Draw instructions to counsel to settle pleadings.			
1.3.3.2 Draw case to counsel to advise, in particular to advise on merits and to advise on evidence.			
1.3.3.3 Draw brief to counsel on interlocutory hearing and on trial.			
1.3.4 Draw up orders.			
1.3.5 Attend on interlocutory hearing with solicitor/ counsel.			
1.3.6 Obtain/oppose judgement under Order 14.			
1.3.7 Negotiations - opportunity to observe conduct of negotiations.			
1.3.8 Attending on taxation of costs.			
1.3.9 Enforcement proceedings.			

AREA OF PRACTICE	✔	ENTER A BRIEF COMMENTARY OF THE SKILLS GAINED; DETAIL THE WORK COMPLETED AND THE FREQUENCY WITH WHICH THE SKILLS WERE PRACTISED OR OBSERVED	DETAILS OF SUPERVISOR
1.4 Patents County Court			
1.4.1 Draft summons and statement of case.			
1.4.2 Draft defence, counterclaim and statement of case.			
1.4.3 Attend before judge on preliminary consideration.			
1.4.4 Attend hearing with solicitor/counsel.			
1.4.5 Negotiations - opportunity to observe conduct of negotiations.			
1.4.6 Drafting a bill of costs for taxation.			
1.4.7 Attending on taxation of costs.			
1.5 Construing a patent and advising on infringement and validity.			
1.6 Gathering evidence			
1.6.1 Collecting examples of infringement, eg buy infringing goods, obtain catalogues, etc.			
1.6.2 Instructing a market research organisation.			
1.6.3 Commissioning a prior art search.			
1.6.4 Preparing proof of evidence of witness.			
1.6.5 Preparing affidavit evidence for interlocutory proceedings.			
1.6.6 Obtaining company searches, trade mark searches and registered design searches.			
1.7 Discovery			
1.7.1 Considering and/or advising on scope of discovery.			
1.7.2 Considering confidentiality restrictions.			
1.7.3 Considering privilege.			
1.7.4 Preparing list of documents.			
1.8 Interim Relief - attending application for:			
1.8.1 Interlocutory injunction.			
1.8.2 Mareva injunction.			
1.8.3 Anton Piller injunction.			

95

AREA OF PRACTICE	✓	ENTER A BRIEF COMMENTARY OF THE SKILLS GAINED; DETAIL THE WORK COMPLETED AND THE FREQUENCY WITH WHICH THE SKILLS WERE PRACTISED OR OBSERVED	DETAILS OF SUPERVISOR
NON CONTENTIOUS		**SECTION TWO**	
2.1 Intellectual Property aspects of corporate transactions:			
2.1.1 Drafting IP clauses in corporate documents.			
2.1.2 Considering and advising on IP provisions in Corporate documents and transactions.			
2.1.3 Advising or drafting transfer of IP.			
2.2 Employees and Consultants			
2.2.1 Drafting employment and consultancy agreements or advising on the IP aspects of such agreements.			
2.2.2 Drafting clauses regarding ownership of Intellectual Property, eg patents, copyright, etc.			
2.2.3 Drafting clauses protecting trade secrets and confidential information.			
2.2.4 Drafting assignment of IP rights from employee/ consultant to employer.			
2.3			
2.3.1 Drafting Licence Agreement			
2.3.2 Drafting Franchise Agreement			
2.3.3 Drafting Distribution Agreement			
2.4 Using patent claims form to ensure that patent does not infringe previous ones. "Construing a patent and advising an infringement and validity."			
2.5 Advising on Broadcasting and Telecommunications law.			
2.6 Computers			
2.6.1 Drafting or advising on contract for sale of computer hardware.			

AREA OF PRACTICE	✔	ENTER A BRIEF COMMENTARY OF THE SKILLS GAINED; DETAIL THE WORK COMPLETED AND THE FREQUENCY WITH WHICH THE SKILLS WERE PRACTISED OR OBSERVED	DETAILS OF SUPERVISOR
2.6.2 Drafting lease of computer hardware. 2.6.3 Drafting software licence. 2.6.4 Advising on computer aspects of corporate transactions. 2.6.5 Attending/carrying out contract negotiations. 2.7 Intellectual Property Licensing Agreements. —			

THE LAW SOCIETY

Wills & Probate Checklist

Name of Trainee Solicitor	
Name of Training Principal/Supervisor/s	
Period over which experience in this area of law gained	

This sample checklist may assist trainee solicitors and training principals to meet their obligations under the Training Contract and Training Code.

You should use the checklist as follows:

1. The legal topic has been broken down into a number of broad sections. You should tick whether you have gained experience in a particular area and then give a brief commentary on the skills gained in each area. (see example below).

2. It is recognised that it can be difficult to incorporate a record of practice support skills and if you find this is the case then you can complete the general practice support skills section at the end of the checklist.

3. A summary of the skills standards can be found under **section 8.1.**

4. The checklist is only a sample. Training Establishments are free to amend or supplement as necessary.

The following broad examples may assist:

Examples of Skills gained

a) **Communication Skills - Wills**
Attending clients to give advice and obtain instructions for Wills. Ascertaining their concerns and factors relevant to them. Gauging approach according to the client and in particular, their physical and mental capacities. Completing attendance notes. Where necessary explaining provisions orally and in writing. Proof reading Wills.

b) **Drafting - Wills**
Drafting Wills, letters and reports to effect the clients wishes and address their concerns. Using, amending and adapting precedent clauses and letters from text books and in-house computer system as appropriate.

c) **Interviewing/Advising**
Attending personal representatives and beneficiaries of estates. Preparing for the interviews by checking firms data base for information and reviewing all documents/file relevant to the matter. Assessing their concerns, priorities and ability to deal with the matter. Advising, guiding and reassuring as necessary, extracting necessary information and agreeing upon courses of action. Making notes, confirming instructions and action required. Attending clients to explain Oaths and other forms. Assessing when appropriate to raise other matters with clients and beneficiaries, in particular to include their Wills, Powers of Attorney and fiscal circumstances.

AREA OF PRACTICE	✓	ENTER A BRIEF COMMENTARY OF THE SKILLS GAINED; DETAIL THE WORK COMPLETED AND THE FREQUENCY WITH WHICH THE SKILLS WERE PRACTISED OR OBSERVED	DETAILS OF SUPERVISOR
WILLS		SECTION ONE	
1.1 Attending client, giving advice and subsequently taking instructions for a Will. Taking note of, inter alia, capacity, domicile, general intent and feasibility having regard to tax planning; exemptions and relief for Inheritance Tax; implications of the Inheritance Tax (Provision for Family and Dependants) Act 1975; Professional/lay Executors; guardians as appropriate.			
1.2 Drafting to include knowledge of all general administrative provisions including charging clauses/ use of precedents.			
1.3 Execution to include advising upon the effects of the Will and miscellaneous points: safe custody, effect of subsequent marriage as appropriate. Safe keeping and updating.			
1.4 Drafting of Codicils.			
PROBATE		SECTION TWO	
2.1 Initial attendance and general advice upon appropriate Grant of Representation to include advice on the provisions of the Will, the implication of the Inheritance Tax (Provision for Family and Dependants) Act 1975 and on Intestacy rules as appropriate and preliminary ascertainment of size and sources of the Estate.			
2.2 Collation of assets and liabilities comprising the Estate including aspects of valuation.			

Area of Practice	✓	Enter a brief commentary of the skills gained; detail the work completed and the frequency with which the skills were practised or observed	Details of Supervisor
2.3 Affidavits of due execution and plight and condition as appropriate.			
2.4 Preparation of Inland Revenue Account to include Inheritance Tax calculations, consideration of available reliefs and exemptions, arrangements for paying Inheritance Tax and possibility of paying by instalments.			
2.5 Preparation of Oath for Executors/Administrators.			
2.6 Attendance upon client with papers before Commissioner for Oaths.			
2.7 Effect Statutory Advertisements pursuant to Section 27 of the Trustee Act.			
2.8 Lodging papers at Principal Probate Registry or District Registry to include personal attendance at Principal Registry (where appropriate).			
2.9 General administrative steps to include registration of Grant, calling in of assets, discharging liabilities, tracing beneficiaries and payment of legacies.			
2.10 General accounting procedures.			
2.11 Consideration of investment to include dealing with share portfolios and other investments.			
2.12 Consideration of tax implications and possible application of Deed of Variation; settlement of Inheritance Tax, Capital Gains Tax and Income Tax (down to the date of death			

AREA OF PRACTICE	✓	ENTER A BRIEF COMMENTARY OF THE SKILLS GAINED; DETAIL THE WORK COMPLETED AND THE FREQUENCY WITH WHICH THE SKILLS WERE PRACTISED OR OBSERVED	DETAILS OF SUPERVISOR
and during course of Administration).			
2.13 Negotiating with Shares Valuation Division of the Capital Taxes Office.			
2.14 Negotiating with the District Valuer over the values of properties.			
2.15 Applying for clearance certificates from the Capital Taxes Office.			
2.16 Preparation of final Administration Accounts, obtaining approval thereto and effecting final distribution.			
2.17 Raising the question of Wills with Beneficiaries where appropriate.			
2.18 Powers of Attorney			

Professional Training Loan Schemes

Barclays Bank plc

You can obtain an information pack and application form from most high street branches of Barclays Bank. Alternatively, you can request one from:

    Barclays Bank plc
    Consumer Lending Section
    PSMD PO Box 120
    Longwood Close
    Westwood Business Park
    Coventry CV4 8JN
    Tel: 024 7669 4242

HSBC

The LPC, the CPE and the Postgraduate Diploma in Law all qualify for the HSBC's postgraduate and professional studies loan. You must, however, transfer your main bank account to this Bank.

   You can apply to borrow up to £5,000 or two-thirds of your salary earned in the 12 months prior to comencement of the course, whichever is the greater. Payment of the loan to you can be negotiated with the Bank and interest is charged at 1 per cent above the HSBC's base rate and is, therefore, variable. Provided you stick to the terms of the loan, you will not be asked to make repayments until 12 months after the end of the course. Repayment of the loan is then by arrangement with the Bank and will include the accumulated interest.

Application forms are available at any branch, but specific queries about the loan scheme can be put to the Chancery Lane branch at:

123 Chancery Lane
London WC2A 1QH
Tel: (020) 7404 4792

National Westminster Bank plc

This offers the popular Professional Trainee Loan Scheme, but you must have a NatWest current account and intend to study on a full-time basis to qualify. You can apply as soon as you have secured a place on the LPC, CPE or Postgraduate Diploma in Law.

Loans of up to £15,000 are available and you have up to 10 years to repay the loan. No repayment is required until at least six months after the end of the course. Interest is charged at a fixed preferential rate. Ask your branch for the rate applicable when you apply.

NatWest has come to an agreement with the Trainee Solicitors' Group, with the Law Society's support, to offer special loan facilities to LPC students who have already accepted an offer of a training contract. Information about this can be requested by telephoning NatWest PRIMELINE on 0345 555000.

Royal Bank of Scotland

This offers its own Career Development Loan Scheme lending up to 80 per cent of course fees up to a maximum of £8,000 and at a low government-subsidised interest rate. This loan is also available if you are studying on a part-time basis. Further information and application forms are available by telephoning freephone 0800 121127, or from:

Commercial Banking Services (Marketing)
PO Box 31
42 St Andrew Square
Edinburgh
EN2 2YE

Lloyds Bank plc/TSB

Lloyds TSB offers a maximum of £10,000 (or two-thirds of your present salary if that is a larger amount) at a fixed interest rate, repayable from six months after the course finished over a period of five years. To be eligible, you must be between 18 and 35 years of age and have been accepted for a place on the LPC. If your loan application is approved, you must move your current bank account to Lloyds TSB. Application forms are available at most branches.

CROSS! Task Force Model Contract Clause

(see 5.13)

This clause has been drafted as a short-term measure for use when trainees and assistant solicitors are faced with the prospect of signing a contract in which the employer reserves (expressly or by default) the right to sue the employee for negligence.

IMPORTANT

THESE CLAUSES ARE PROVIDED ON THE BASIS THAT THEY ARE GOVERNED BY ENGLISH LAW.

THEY ARE FOR USE IN ENGLAND AND WALES ONLY IN CONTRACTS GOVERNED BY ENGLISH LAW ONLY.

THEY SHOULD NOT BE USED WITHOUT SEEKING LEGAL ADVICE.

ALL LIABILITY ON THE PART OF The Freelance Solicitors' Group, The Young Solicitors' Group and The Trainee Solicitors' Group, The CROSS! Task Force and the Authors IS, SAVE FOR PERSONAL INJURY OR DEATH, HEREBY EXCLUDED TO THE FULLEST EXTENT PERMITTED BY LAW.

- Save where the result of any malicious, dishonest, fraudulent or criminal act or omission on the part of the [Consultant/Employee]:—
  a. the Principal will indemnify the [Consultant/Employee] against all liability arising or claims made by any person (including the Principal), and
  b. to the extent of—
- any deductible payable by the Principal pursuant to the Solicitors' Indemnity Rules,
- any top-up insurance cover taken out by the Principal, and
- any other unindemnified or uninsured losses incurred by the Principal, including, without limitation, other indemnity or insurance deductibles or excesses, excess liability (over any limits) and any claims or premium loading the [Consultant/Employee] shall not be liable to the Principal (and the Principal hereby waives any claim against the [Consultant/Employee]) as a result of anything done or omitted to be done by the [Consultant/Employee] in the provision of the Services by the [Consultant/Employee] in the course of the [Consultant's contract/Employee's employment].
- the [Consultant/Employee] shall not make any admission of liability nor make any offer, promise or settlement relating to any claim which falls within the provisions of this clause without the written consent of the Principal.

Other Useful Addresses and Telephone Numbers

ACAS:	London	(020) 7396 5100
	Midlands	(0115) 969 3355
	Northern	(0113) 243 1371
	North West	(0161) 228 3222
		(0151) 427 8881
	South West	(0117) 974 4066
		(01252) 811868
	Wales	(029) 2076 1126

The Association of African Caribbean & Asian Lawyers
114 Chancery Lane
London WC2A 1PQ
Tel: (020) 7320 5873

The Association of Women Solicitors
Contact: Judith Willis
Tel: (020) 7320 5793
Maternity Helpline: (020) 8676 9887

BLS Professional Development
Denning House
1 Hazelhurst Road
Worsley
Manchester M28 2SX
Tel: (0161) 728 1778
Fax: (0161) 728 3778

Central Law Training Limited
Wrens Court
52–54 Victoria Road
Sutton Coldfield
Birmingham B71 1SX
Tel: (0121) 355 0900
Fax: (0121) 355 5517

Chambers & Partners — A Guide to the Legal Profession: Student Edition
23 Long Lane
London EC1A 9ET
Tel: (020) 7606 1300
Fax: (020) 7606 0906

The Citizenship Foundation
15 St Swithens Lane
London EC4N 5AL
Tel: (020) 7929 3344
Fax: (020) 7929 0922
www.citfou.org.uk

Council for Licensed Conveyancers
16 Glebe Road
Chelmsford
Essex CM1 1QG
Tel: (01245) 349599
Fax: (01245) 341300

CPE Applications Board
PO Box 84
Guildford
Surrey GU3 1YX
Tel: (01483) 451080

Crown Prosecution Service
50 Ludgate Hill
London EC4M 7EX
Tel: (020) 7796 8000
Fax: (020) 7796 8161

General Council of the Bar
1 Bedford Row
Gray's Inn
London WC1R 4DB
Tel: (020) 7252 0082
Fax: (020) 7831 9217

General Council of the Bar
Education and Training Officer
2–3 Cursitor Street
London EC4A 1NE
Tel: (020) 7440 4000
Fax: (020) 7440 4002

Institute of Legal Executives
Kempston Manor
Kempston
Bedford MK42 7AB
Tel: (01234) 841000
Fax: (01234) 840373

Institute of Paralegal Training
Clymping Street
Clymping
Littlehampton
West Sussex BN17 5RN
Tel: (01903) 714276
Fax: (01903) 713710

Law Careers Advice Network
Student Line: (0870) 606 2555
LawCareers.Net (www.LawCareers.Net)

Law Centres Federation
Duches House
18–19 Warren Street
London W1P 5DB
Tel: (020) 7387 8570
Fax: (020) 7387 8368

Legal Action Group
242 Pentonville Road
London N1 9UN
Tel: (020) 7833 2931
Fax: (020) 7837 6094

Legal Practice Course Central Applications Board
PO Box 84
Guildford
Surrey GU3 1YX
Tel: (01483) 301282
www.lawcabs.ac.uk

National Association of Citizens' Advice Bureaux (CAB)
115–123 Pentonville Road
London EC1V 2QN
Tel: (020) 7833 2181
Fax: (020) 7833 4371

The Office for the Supervision of Solicitors
(including Discrimination/Bullying Helpline)
Victoria Court
8 Dormer Place
Leamington Spa
Warwickshire CV32 5AE
Tel: (01926) 820082
Fax: (01926) 431435

SolCare Helpline for Alcoholic Solicitors
Contact: Barry Pritchard
Tel: (01766) 512222

INDEX